MW00573154

What people are saying about
Soul Cats

"*Soul Cats* is a tender and heart-pawing journey of care. It's a reminder that when we stop pushing for what we want, we create a space that can be filled by love. Tamara and her council of wise feline companions take you on a beautiful journey of healing. Get ready to discover…"
—**Stephen Mulhearn**, Director Lendrick Lodge Retreat Scotland

"*Soul Cats* is one of the most inspiring books I have ever come across. It will make you cry, it will make you smile and it will open your heart as only the love of animals can do. Kudos to Tamara for this beautiful work!"
—**Lucia Giovannini**, Bestselling author of *A Whole New Life: Discover the Power of Positive Transformation* and inspirational speaker

"Recognizing meaningful connections to all our animal relatives since time immemorial Tamara invites us to reconnect with these practices and to explore our own very possible and deep journeys with our own animal relatives. We are witnesses as she chronicles her egoless journey as she authentically listens to the voice, spirit and needs of her furry relatives. I want to be her cat!"
—**Maria A. Trevizo**, Indigenous Elder, Auntie, Sister, Mother

"*Soul Cats* is an inspiring, informative guide for understanding, connecting with, and supporting our feline companions, and in turn letting them to touch and feed our souls."
—**Jim Dickie,** Trustee Emeritus, Morris Animal Foundation

"*Soul Cats* is a true lesson in love, wisdom, compassion, and harmony for all those who have the consciousness to open their hearts and minds to embrace the spirit and interconnection of all living souls."
—**Fiona Oakes,** Founder of Tower Hill Stables Animal Sanctuary, Essex, UK

SOUL CATS

How Feline Friends Teach Us to Live From the Heart

TAMARA SCHENK

Made for Success Publishing
P.O. Box 1775 Issaquah, WA 98027
www.MadeForSuccessPublishing.com

Distributed by Made for Success Publishing

Cover: Bill Jeckells, Graphic Design, UK
Translation: Bernhard and Susannah Sulzer, A Great Translation, USA

First Printing

Library of Congress Cataloging-in-Publication data
Schenk, Tamara
    SOUL CATS: How Feline Friends Teach Us to Live From the Heart

        p. cm.

LCCN: 2021949450
ISBN: 978-1-64146-683-7 (*Paperback*)
ISBN: 978-1-64146-684-4 (*eBook*)
ISBN: 978-1-64146-685-1 (*Audiobook*)

Printed in the United States of America

For further information contact Made for Success Publishing
+14255266480 or email service@madeforsuccess.net

Contents

INTRODUCTION

Congratulations! I am glad that your intuition guided you and my *Soul Cats* book found its way to you. I wish you many exciting moments with Max, Flix, and Howy as our story unfolds. May my book provide you much joy and enrich your life with some inspiration and experiences that will deepen your relationship with your feline friends.

The book's creation is a very special story. You might already have read on the back cover that it is Max's assignment for me. Soul cat Max's assignment to be exact; it's the story of Max and Flix, and later of Howy as well. It is inextricably linked to my own story and my transformation.

Soul Cats is more than just an account of our three senior cats, adopted from the animal shelter. It's precisely the "more" that is so important to Max and me: understanding and accepting animals as fully recognized family members, as intelligent, sensitive living beings with unique wisdom and emotions. With their own personality, as individuals with particular needs.

Max, who dictated the closing remarks to me, said it very clearly: "Never stop helping animals and creating more understanding of animals among humans. And that is why *Soul Cats* is so important."

Max initiated our story and I couldn't be more grateful for everything that unfolded since I met him. All the beautiful moments, the unconditional love, the timeless bond, and also all the challenges I encountered. Yes, even tough challenges are always an opportunity to learn and grow. That's the way I learned to look at things. At the same time, our story is a story of tremendous growth and transformation for my cats and myself.

I experienced how important it is to let things happen and to remain open for all that develops. This requires an open heart, patience, intuition, and time. And it especially requires a lot of love and acceptance that things can turn out differently than you might have imagined. Maybe you will experience even more joy together than you would have ever thought possible. Most probably your bond to your cat will grow much deeper than you expected. Maybe you will need to overcome a few challenges. Max, Flix, and Howy have quite a lot to say about all those topics.

Some animals, particularly the ones from an animal shelter, often experienced horrible things. They come with a lot of "baggage" and some of their "baggage" might resonate in one way or another with your own past. They need trust, love, time and patience; and clarity at the same time. And, they need the certainty that once they arrive, they will be given the time they require to heal, and that this will be their forever home as family members; that you'll be there for them even when it becomes difficult. Flix's and Howy's stories will provide a lot of insight, which includes the paths we traveled together.

When we take animals into our home, we take on responsibility. Responsibility for their lives. Because the moment you take an animal into your home, his or her life depends on your choices. It might sound a bit hard for you. But ultimately, that's exactly what it is. Because you decide, for example, which food you give to your animal. You decide how much space your animal has, how many places to scratch, hide or sleep it receives. In the case of cats, whether or not they go outside or not. You decide whether and what kind of treatment you will provide when your animal gets sick, traumatized, or develops behavioral challenges. You decide to what degree you want to familiarize yourself with certain topics, such as chronic diseases, which in my situation we were dealing with. It's all your choice—and your responsibility.

You may also decide how the end of your animal's life will occur. From my point of view, it is important to deal with this before the situation occurs. Death seems to be one of society's last taboo topics, in regard to humans as well as animals. I tell it here as it is, no glossing over things. In particular, I describe how I acted in two such situations, which were very different from each other. Overall, the experience of accompanying animals on this final path was very enriching and fulfilling. This experience deepened our bond even more, across time and space. Forever. And no, I personally am no longer afraid of death.

Max gave me his assignment for this book a few weeks before his death. After his move to Rainbowland, I wrote half of the book within a few months. Then Max sent us our beloved Howy, and for a while, I was too busy to write. You'll read soon why that was. Then I wasn't sure for a long time whether the book would be about Max and Flix, or about Max, Flix, and Howy. It became the latter because Howy told me so. I then finished the book in less than four weeks.

Now it is time to say thank you to all the wonderful humans whom I met, with and through the soul cats, who helped us in many different ways.

A heartfelt thank you goes to Sylvia Rassloff who showed me ways to communicate with animals, taught me animal communication, and who accompanied Max and Flix for a long time. During my animal communication training, I met wonderful women: Kristin and Kerstin. We helped each other out with our animals and are still doing that today.

At the same time, I have also invested much time into learning about energetic work. A heartfelt thank you goes to my teacher Toby Alexander, who showed me his approach and taught me various methods and processes regarding auric clearing, karma clearing, DNA activation, and trauma healing at the quantum level. This inspired me to build my business "Energy Field Mastery" where I follow my mission to help people to leverage their full potential and to heal the human/animal relationship.

In addition, I want to thank the team at the Hofheim Veterinary Clinic deeply for treating our soul cats from the beginning in a very involved way, with great competence and success. All three soul cats had various crises which they wouldn't have survived without help from the Hofheim Veterinary Clinic. Little Flix, after years of contemplation, even found it quite alright to have his blood pressure taken while sitting in the cardiologist's lap!

A big thank you goes to Tom Kaetzke and his practice for animal health. Without his help, Howy wouldn't have overcome his chronic illnesses as effectively, and Flix also benefitted significantly from the traditional Chinese medicine (TCM) and bioresonance therapy, always based on conventional medical diagnosis and therapy.

I want to also extend my gratefulness to all the other wonderful "Cat Mums" and "Cat Dads" I met along the way, who took this path with us in various ways. Many thanks go to all you amazing human beings who I can't list here individually. But you know who you are! Thank you from the bottom of my heart.

Resources to contact during crises are very important. Knowing where to turn when you don't know what to do is critical. And, we experienced such situations. Exchanging experiences, receiving advice and recommendations regarding vets, therapies, and methods can make all the difference. Often it's even more important to simply have someone listening when you're quite emotional about something.

I am very grateful to the Mainz Animal Shelter where we met Max and Flix and learned to love them; and to the Hanau Animal Shelter where Howy lived when we met him. And a very special thank you to Howy's contact person at the shelter, our dear Martina Frank, who put Howy in touch with us and stays in contact to this day.

Last but not least, I want to express my gratitude to Bernhard and Susannah Sulzer from "A Great Translation" who translated my book into English with lots of cat sense.

Finally, I am super grateful being pointed to Made for Success in Seattle, an amazing, dedicated company that processed all the many, many workstreams in the background to prepare *Soul Cats* to be launched in the English-speaking market. Their dedication to *Soul Cats* and to do whatever they can to make the book a success is impressive.

The whole team works like an amazing clockwork, and my special thanks go to Bryan Heathman whom I met via my friend and author Helen Yu (thank you my friend), Deedee Heathman for her amazing "book cat herding" success, and Lennie Martin for her fantastic "cat sense" and precision regarding language and style while editing *Soul Cats*.

And thanks a million to Michael, my husband, the world's best #catdad.

And now, I wish you great joy with the soul cats!

MAX'S ASSIGNMENT

There's a reason why you are holding this book in your hands, or are looking at it through your Reader. Max made the following request: Max wanted me to write a book about soul cats, about our deep relationship, a book featuring him as the main character, and with Flix, his friend, and with Howy, whom he sent to us later. But we'll get to that; let's do one thing at a time.

Whoever had the great fortune to know Max personally will understand immediately why his wish was my command. OK, I also like writing. But Max knew that as well ...

So, the assignment to write a book came about this way:

It was a few weeks before he died, when one beautiful evening, he jumped on the living room table. He hardly ever did that because he didn't like books and magazines piled up, which was often the case on our table. We make sure to keep the house clean in many places, especially for Max, but the living room table isn't necessarily part of it.

There was a special reason causing him to jump up on the table that evening. It was the beautiful book *Soul Dogs,* by Severine Martens, which was lying on the table.

As is mostly the case when things are really supposed to happen and are meant for you, the universe is lending a mighty hand—as in this case. Because this wonderful book, which I had just been enjoying so much, was lying in the middle of the living room table. And Max walked straight toward it and sat down on top of it.

I said to him: "Max, do you want to have a soul cats book?" He only looked at me, his expression very certain, as always when he was serious about something, and then took off again.

"I hope she understood me," is what he was probably thinking to himself. "Humans … I can't make it any clearer to them … "

Only after his death, I understood how many messages and assignments he had left for me and how much he had arranged before his death, with one clear goal in mind: that I wouldn't fall into a deep hole and succumb to devastating sorrow. He always wanted to see me laugh, be happy, and savor every moment. The latter seems to be a core message by animals for us humans.

When I was sad or even had to cry, he always felt like taking care of me more than any other time; snuggled up to me, comforted me and gave me his love and support, even though he really needed all his strength for himself. But that's how he was, our Max. Soul cat. Solid as a rock. Best friend to all. An incredibly wise soul.

He really always felt responsible; for me, for us and especially for his friend Flix, with whom he came to us in January 2015 from the animal shelter.

Maybe we should start at the beginning, when Max had adopted us, and he and Flix moved in with us.

January 10, 2015,
When Everything Began ...

I had always wanted to live with animals again. I grew up with animals, mainly with dogs. I rode horses for many years and have a special bond with horses. You always find dogs in horse barns, and of course cats as well.

Throughout my professional life, I traveled a lot; more and more really. And at the same time, I had less and less contact with animals. That was not a good development for me. Step by step, I changed that. First, I got out of the consulting profession, for which I normally had to travel four days a week. Michael also had to travel a lot and still does today. I could not in good conscience care for an animal—no matter what type—that way.

Gradually, I changed my professional life in a way that my work is very enjoyable, and I can carry it out mostly from home. A classic win-win situation! As I was the only European member of an American research team, it didn't matter at all where I carried out my work. I only had to be online. As soon as I had become comfortable in that role, I knew I wanted animals again in my life; preferably cats; yes, cats, plural. It's probably more pleasant for animals to have a partner of the same species when living with humans.

It was clear from the beginning that we wanted to offer cats from the animal shelter a chance to have a loving home--ideally, those velvet paws which didn't stand much of a chance to ever leave the animal shelter. With this conviction, we arrived, on January 10, 2015, at the Mainz Animal Shelter. Yes, we wanted to adopt two cats; gladly, somewhat older animals.

We were given a tour and then were shown the cat dwelling, where Max and Flix lived. Max was in charge of the cat dwelling. It was immediately obvious. And, he was interested in us right away, especially in me. Max and I had a great connection from the start. Within moments, he let me touch him and stroke his beautiful red fur. He was snuggling up to me almost immediately. Or, you could say he wasn't shy at all throwing himself at me!

It was quite obvious that he felt comfortable with me. And where was Flix, the other half of the duo? Then, his name was still Felix. He hid in the back of the cat dwelling, curled up on the heater. He was a very sweet, significantly smaller, black and white tomcat. It took quite a while before he let me approach him, but touching ... please don't!

Max kept his eyes on us, watching us intently as we checked out Flix and got closer to him. I then returned to the front part of the cat dwelling where Max was waiting. Michael stayed in the back with Flix. We read the background information on both: 2000 and 2003 were the estimated birth years. They were both picked up by members of the shelter at a feeding station. More wasn't known about their past. Oh, and Max was suffering from early stage of chronic kidney disease (CKD), a chronic kidney deficiency. But, it could be treated with specially selected food. Well, then ... sometimes it's right to just daringly follow one's heart without knowing all the details in advance.

"Well, do you dig everything then?" Max seemed to ask. He walked toward me, very friendly, when I returned. And then he sat upon on my purse, which I had put down on the floor.

A clear signal! "Come on, get the paperwork done so we can leave," he seemed to say. I looked at Michael. He looked at me. I understood I would go ahead and take care of the paperwork, so we could take these two wonderful souls home with us.

I had a conversation with a manager of the shelter. I had to answer a few questions about my experience with and knowledge about cats, as well as regarding our house and the available space. We also discussed questions aimed at the sufficient time we would spend with the cats, the required financial means, and who would take care of them when we would be traveling or if unforeseen situations arose. It seemed I was able to answer all the questions satisfactorily. I paid the protection fee and signed the contract to adopt them.

Then I went back to Max and Flix to put them both in the XXL cat carrier. Max went in right away. Flix seemed encouraged by that to follow along, with a little help.

With both in the carrier and enough food for the weekend, we went home with Max, 12, and Flix, 15 (the ages the shelter had estimated) to their forever home. They would never again have to worry about anything.

ARRIVING AT HOME

We had no problems on the drive home. Max seemed to protect Flix. Flix lay curled up in the darkest corner of the carrier and was almost invisible. And, Max was observing closely where we were driving.

When we arrived home, we opened the carrier, and the two cats came out very slowly and carefully. Max went straight into my office behind the red sofa, and Flix fled under the sofa in the living room. They stayed there for a while. We wanted to show them their litter boxes, one downstairs and one upstairs, but there was no time for that. They first seemed to need some rest and to get familiar with the new surroundings. After a while, they tiptoed out from their hiding places and discovered the litter boxes themselves.

They tried some food in the evening—at least to check if the basic food supply from the new service staff was working. And it seemed to be OK. In any case, the tigers were surveying everything very carefully. Max didn't seem to be familiar with open staircase steps. He bravely went upstairs and looked at me from above, as if saying: "Really? And now I'm supposed to get back down?" Flix in the meantime was checking out the situation in a crouched stance. It seemed to go quite well. Then they retreated back into their hiding places.

Flix was amazingly swift, dashed around all corners and as quickly as possible sprinted back into his hiding place. That's how Felix became simply Flix—short and swift.

We were facing the first night in the new home. Let's put it this way: no one got much sleep, neither the two-legged nor the four-legged occupants. Our dear cats must have visited a few of their litter boxes at least ten times. And, we were very happy to have the two of them with us, although very nervous trying to do everything correctly. The two cats had stolen our hearts within one day and weren't going to let go; beautiful, but also very exciting. From now on, we were responsible for their lives and their happiness.

DEVELOPING A ROUTINE

We spent the next days getting to know each other better. For the first two weeks, in the morning, both stayed mostly in their hiding spots. They only came out for breakfast, then hid again to only come back out in the afternoon. They were most active in the evening. Walking around, surveying the new territory, and getting to know the people. It's very important to give the animals the time they need to adjust. They decide when and how they will approach their human caretakers. Who knows what they had to endure in the past. It all takes time. Their time. Giving them that time builds trust.

We needed to learn about their feeding schedule and get to know their various likings. Max, for example, was seeking to be close to someone. Flix was much more careful, shy as well as fearful. Only little by little, he allowed me to touch and stroke him.

Eating occurred in many little increments. Max was always immediately interested in his food as soon as it was served, and took a bite. He was on a diet for his kidney condition. For the moment, we stayed with that food. He seemed to like it. Later on, we added high-quality wet food for senior cats. He ate really well from the start. It was completely different with Flix. At first, he seemed not to be interested at all. He ignored especially the wet food. But, as soon as he heard the crackling sound of dry food, he was unleashed--Flix, the dry food junkie. It took many months of effort until we had accustomed him to high-quality wet food, but more about that in the chapter "Flix, Dry-food Junkie."

They were as different with regard to eating as they were regarding everything else. Max was the boss. Flix was thankful when Max had surveyed everything and found it acceptable. Then he felt safe and followed Max's example. Their ways of playing were just as different. Max wasn't really interested at all. Why chase a piece of yarn? "Well, OK, if I catch it and can hold on to it, then yes," he seemed to say. This didn't seem dignified enough for Max.

Flix, on the other hand, loved to play from the start. Whenever he could keep himself occupied by playing, he perked up. He forgot for a few moments how scared he usually was.

Most exciting for Flix was chasing a string around a table leg. It was such a joyous riot for him. Wonderful! Every time, we enjoyed it tremendously ourselves!

Both cats adjusted well during the first two months. Together, we developed routines. Eating, playing, snuggling; just important things for cats. After a while, they dared enter the bedroom. Only very carefully at first, to see whether or not the service staff was still alive and the food supply still secured. Then they became braver and, with Max leading the way, ventured out more forcefully. The initially hesitant attempts to jump on the bed became daily rituals in order to wake up the staff and to snuggle a little. Max, weighing about 13 pounds, was anything but a feather when getting comfortable on my stomach. He also liked to lie down and stretch in the middle of the bed. At first, when he noticed that Michael wasn't here during the week, Max became used to making himself comfortable on that side of the bed. When Michael came home for the weekend, Max sat on the bed very self-assured and looked at him as if he were saying: "Well, I don't know where you actually plan to sleep, but this here is my spot."

Only when he became very ill did he move over to my side, and slept most of the night snuggled in my arm. We were refueling on love. What he had been missing most in his former life, he could now absorb in excess. And, he really enjoyed it tremendously—and so did I.

Contrary to Max who spent a lot of time on his visits to the bedroom, Flix preferred short visits. He did announce them though: "I am here now, hellooooooo," followed by quick steps around the left and right side of the bed, also with vocal accompaniments. He was obviously weighing several criteria that would have to be considered before deciding on the appropriate spot from which to jump onto the bed. Most of the time, both shared the bed very well as partial territory. Nevertheless, Max sometimes had the urge to show Flix who was boss and chased him away; short and sweet, with a bat of his paw. Poor Flix would then take off, very perturbed. I always tried to explain to them that there is enough room for both and, most importantly, even more love.

But, the time came when I needed to travel to the US for a few days, and the two of them had to be looked after by someone else for the first time. I quickly found a neighbor who had cats herself. She agreed to feed both in the morning and at night, and to play with them as well.

With a heavy heart, I went on my trip. The two cats reacted very differently to that. Max didn't seem to mind it a bit. But Flix was not at all OK with it. Old fears seemed to well up inside of him; he threw up at least twice while I was gone. As soon as one of us humans was back with them, things went significantly better. Flix's problem with vomiting would continue through all of the first year, until we found out what caused it, and then we were able to help him.

Leaving them was very tough for me. When I got to the airport, I already missed them. I sat in the lounge with tears in my eyes, waiting for my flight.

Never had I looked forward so much to coming back home. Max and Flix felt exactly the same. Being together was the best thing in the world.

CAT TREE WITH A VIEW

Scratching posts and scratching utensils are essential for cats. The little tigers have to scratch for various reasons: to maintain their claws and to mark their territory. Especially, indoor cats need various options to fulfill their scratching urges.

At the very beginning, we bought a cat condo that offered entries on three different levels. We thought that was fantastic. Those were great places to hide. Yet, Max and Flix at first ignored it completely. After a while, they used it on the outside in order to maintain their claws and to stretch their whole bodies. Only much later both discovered that they could simply climb up and sit on top of it. Jumping up on the condo in a very elegant way wasn't a problem for Flix at all. For Max, weighing almost twice as much as Flix, it was certainly a problem. Not because he couldn't do it. But, more than once he had toppled over the whole condo, and had scared himself and me half to death. Later on, we moved the condo to a different place, close to the sideboard, so that Max could jump across onto the condo in just two steps. That was good for all our nerves.

I also had a smaller cat tree in my study that didn't get much attention either. Max only took to it much later. It was an ideal place to supervise your Cat Mum when she's working. Right at eye-level, so to speak.

I had to get a real cat tree, one with several levels, a cave, and two places to sit. I said it, I ordered it, I got it. And I assembled it. We put it in the living room, on the left side of the window facing the southwest balcony. A spot from which the tigers would have a fantastic view: looking across the apartment, toward the entrance door and also toward the outside.

What I hadn't considered was Max's size compared to the standard size of cat trees. Max inspected the merchandise, climbed up on it, squeezed into the cave and looked at me accusingly. "Don't you see that this is way too small for me?"

But of course; now I saw it too. The standard products were for smaller cats or what you might call "normal" cats. Flix, only weighing about 8 lbs., had a lot of fun with this cat tree the first year. Often, he would sit up on top and look out at the world. In the summer, he liked snuggling up inside the cave to avoid the very bright sunlight. It soon became Flix's own personal cat tree.

I had to get an XXL cat tree for Max. It didn't take me long to find a place to put it. The wicker chair there was really just decoration and could be removed. So getting a cat tree for Max's size turned out to be another good investment. It was absolutely worth the money we spent—very solid, with two different big trays, a big seating shell, one cave, and two boards to sit on; all at different levels, from the floor to the ceiling; a ceiling clamping unit.

His Cat Dad assembled and positioned this cat tree for him. It's hard for me to say who had more fun with it. Even while Cat Dad was still assembling it, Max was already standing next to it, full of great expectations and running back and forth across the many individual parts that were lying there, ready to be put together. Michael really enjoyed assembling this for both little tigers, but especially for Max.

The day the tree would be finished was almost here! What would the two of them do?

The conquest of the cat tree occurred in several phases. First, Max lay down in the lower smaller perch. Of course, that's exactly where he shouldn't because of his weight. You could call it Murphy's law. And Flix jumped with elegance all the way to the top, into the large perch, which was actually designed for Max's weight. It didn't take long until Max discovered the entire tree with all its possibilities.

In true alpha cat fashion, he quickly knocked Flix off the boss's penthouse perch. From that point on, Max was always up there--and only he. Flix wasn't allowed anymore, as long as Max was the boss and was able to defend his position. Later, a few months before his death, the balance of power between the two shifted and Flix, first rather hesitantly but with increasing confidence, took over the boss's seat. That happened calmly, without any fight. Max had planned his resignation and had planned an orderly transfer of duties when it was time, and he felt that he had to actively empower Flix.

Didn't we, I mean didn't Max and Flix, now have enough scratching options? Yes of course, one might think. Only if there hadn't been the shelf next to the cabinet in Michael's office. Somehow, both cats managed to jump from the adjacent shelf onto the closet. Jumping down was accompanied with them hitting the wood floor pretty hard, and I felt sorry for their bones, since they were both seniors.

So we placed a "half-tree" there, a walk-up cabinet for seniors, so to speak. It was used often by both of them during the first year. Flix used the walk-up right away, every time we had guests. That's when he re-experienced his old fears and he fled onto the cabinet. And he stayed there. Other times, he simply had fun jumping on it and viewing the world from up there.

The first year, we often found him sitting on the cabinet in the morning, waiting until the staff was finally ready to serve breakfast. Later, when he had built up his trust, he preferred to come into the bedroom and wake us in order to snuggle, and to make sure that all morning procedures for the cat feeding were started.

Sunbathing for Breakfast

It was mostly Max who turned into a summer sunlight connoisseur. From the first year on, but especially during the second year, he began the day with breakfast on the sunny balcony. A sunbath in the morning couldn't hurt. He expanded his procedure little by little, and eventually became used to making himself comfortable on the garden table to take advantage of the best sunbathing position.

When I arrived on the balcony with my smoothie and cappuccino, Max had stretched out long and was enjoying the sun. Oh, I really enjoyed these moments with him. We snuggled, talked to each other, and began the day together. Quietly, lovingly, peacefully. Those were intimate, trusting moments. And, Max had enjoyed so much sunlight; it seemed enough for vitamin D activation. Not too much and not too little.

At first, he had really admired my breakfast habits. "Green things in a glass? And you want to drink that?" He sniffed it for me very carefully. It wouldn't be to anyone's benefit if the service staff poisoned themselves. Most of the time, he did approve of it. "Well, what can you say? Oh well, people just eat and drink all kinds of weird things." That's what he seemed to think.

When Michael was home, Max was often more interested in Michael's cereal with fresh fruit than my smoothie. Cat Dad's food had to be inspected as well. It was something different again.

The endless inner calm, this inner peace that Max exhibited during these morning moments were wonderful. He taught me a lot about these moments. The acceptance of the moment, the happy feeling in these moments, were an incredible lesson, provided to me on a regular basis by Sir Max.

So we sat in the sun for a few moments. Quietly, blissfully, turned inward, connected, happy. Then we cuddled; Max loved to be caressed. He liked to have his forehead, ears and back rubbed; he thought that was fabulous. As soon as he had enough, he moved into the shade. And I went to my writing desk.

After repeated attempts during the first year to get his kidney inefficiency under control, we visited the veterinary clinic located nearby to get a more comprehensive diagnosis. In any case, due to the ultrasound exam, Max had a shaved underbelly. Because it was the middle of summer, the vet told us not to let him lie in the heat of the sun for more than 20 minutes until the fur had grown back.

And wouldn't you know it, Max already knew about this. Unbelievable, but when he was lying in the sun in a very relaxed manner, having his belly warmed by the morning sun, you could tell time by it. After 20 minutes at the most, he moved into the shade.

That was Max: intelligent, wise, reflective, mostly dominant, and irresistible; just what you would expect from Sir Max.

How Cats Drink–or How They Don't

Much has been written about how to make cats drink. Of course, as desert animals, they prefer to drink only a little, which doesn't make it easier for them during their domesticated life.

So, water bowls (ideally more than one) need to be placed at various spots, but not next to the food. And, a drinking fountain would have miraculous effects, increasing cats' drinking volume up to 30 percent. Running water is also very important to entice cats to drink. It sounds all very logical at first.

Because of Max and his inefficient kidneys, drinking was particularly important. But Max was the one that was hardly seen at the many water stations. And, it was he who needed water the most.

We decided very quickly on a plan. In addition to the water bowls at various places, we had to get a drinking fountain. The first one we bought came highly recommended, regarding effectiveness as well as ease of cleaning. Unfortunately, it looked more like a low bidet. It wouldn't be a problem if both, and especially Max, would drink more. In this regard, Flix is a very smart cat. You can see him drink several times a day. He really does a great job.

To Max, the fountain was part of the territory and had to be inspected. But there was no further interest in the equipment. The looks while the cats were inspecting it carefully clearly conveyed "You really didn't have to get that" and "That thing is still here?" After a few months experience with the first drinking fountain, with Max completely ignoring it, I sold it to someone in the cat CKD group on Facebook.

But, I didn't give up that easily on "project drinking fountain." There had to be a beautiful drinking fountain somewhere that, at the same time, was endearing to the cats. And indeed, there were beautiful ones—of course more expensive—fountains made of ceramic which would at least serve as decent living room decoration if our two tigers wouldn't want to drink from it.

So, we decided to bring the new fountain into the house. It was a great-looking ceramic fountain, cream-colored, with blue cat paws pictured on it. Really nice! When we had it ready to go, the two boys' reaction was very much as before. They were walking around very carefully without paying any further attention to it, or daring to drink from it!

Summer was approaching, and I simply started putting an additional water bowl for each of them on the balcony. Lo and behold, this became Max's preferred ritual: in the morning, Cat Mum was to please open the door to the balcony. Next, we first drink from the water bowls. Then, much refreshed, we turn our attention to breakfast with the service personnel and the sun in the sky.

They say all cats always prefer fresh running water. Not so. Until he became very ill, Max always drank stagnant water. Only later did he learn to appreciate the drinking fountain.

As time went by, I observed that sometimes there was more water missing from the drinking fountain than could be attributed to simple evaporation. I surmise that the two of them had been playing a big joke on us for quite a while, leaving us to believe that the fountain was absolutely uninteresting. But at night, they must have used it nevertheless. At least sometimes ...

Only over the last two months of his life, Max learned to appreciate the drinking fountain. During that time, he ate very little anymore, but drank much more to keep his body functioning. The larger water surface of the fountain seemed to be more attractive to him, and the comfortable height made it so much more accessible than a flat water bowl.

MAX'S CHRONIC KIDNEY DISEASE (CKD)

Max came to us already diagnosed as a CKD[1]-cat. We were told that it wouldn't be a problem, that it can be managed with the right food.

At the shelter, he had been put on a kidney diet. We were told to just let him come to us, get comfortable and then in two or three months have his kidney function tested. That's what the vet at the shelter said to us.

And that's what we did. The first vet we visited with Max tested his kidney function: creatinine, urea, and phosphate. The creatinine level had gone up. Not good. Okay, what can we do about it? A homeopathic therapy called SUC[2] was recommended to us. He should receive it three times a week. How do we administer it? With his food, no problem. Only later did we learn that the content of these ampules is best received through mucous membranes, at least ten minutes apart from any normal feeding. Oh, the teeth were looking bad we were told, lots of tartar. But that couldn't be fixed because of the kidneys.

---

1. According to Wikipedia, CKD is "is a type of kidney disease in which there is gradual loss of kidney function over a period of months to years. Initially there are generally no symptoms; later, symptoms may include leg swelling, feeling tired, vomiting, loss of appetite, and confusion.

2. SUC= homeopathic complex remedy, consisting of Solidago compositum ad us. vet., Ubichinon compositum, Coenzyme compositum ad us. vet.

Unfortunately, some vets seem to just "manage" the disease and to sell the kidney diet as the only cure-all. At the next check-up, Max's kidney function levels were higher again. The vet thought we could try out a new medication, Telmisartan.[1] OK then, let's do that.

I administered the new medication to Max, always in the evening, as prescribed. But my agile Max grew more tired and listless. Something wasn't right. Max was a 13 lb. cat who had neither lost weight nor was suffering from life-threatening depression. I suspected the new medication, but wasn't clear on how everything was interconnected.

And what can I say? You guessed it, his kidney function levels were up again by the next exam. That visit was the last one with this vet because he explained tersely that there was nothing else he could do for Max, and that I had been made aware of the fatal progression of his disease.

Meanwhile, Max eyeballed the vet with an alert and critical look. He looked at me and I looked at him: We're leaving, this second!

OK, let's get out of this practice. I reserved all of the following weekend for reading everything I could find on cats and CKD. With the help of Facebook, I joined a CKD self-help group. Several times, an internist from nearby Hofheim Veterinary Clinic was recommended to me. A few days later, in the evening, we paid them a visit, bringing along a tired but brave Max.

Our new vet was very engaged and made a great effort to do for Max whatever she could. She threw her arms up in horror when she realized how much incompetence, incorrect treatment and lack of empathy we had experienced at the previous vet. Had he ever taken Max's blood pressure? No, he hadn't. Tested his urine? No, he hadn't. But he had prescribed Semintra? That was a big no-no. How right she was.

Max's blood pressure was at 110; that was at the veterinary clinic where one or more dogs were continuously barking somewhere. The vet was very open, direct and thorough. She noticed that I had become familiar with the disease, acknowledging it by explaining everything in detail to me. She compiled a complete, geriatric blood profile, urinary status with sediment

1. Telmisartan (brand names are Semintra or Micardis) is in a class of medications known as the ARBs (angiotensin II receptor blockers). Telmisartan received FDA approval to treat primarily inappropriate urinary protein loss (glomerular disease) in cats. It can also be used to treat high blood pressure. Sources: Veterinary Partner http://www.vin.com; Tanya's Comprehensive Guide to Feline Chronic Kidney Disease, https://www.felinecrf.org

study, ultrasound, and blood pressure measurement. She took ninety minutes to arrive at a correct and clear diagnosis.

It became obvious very quickly that I had found a very competent vet who would steer everything in the right direction. Max should never have received the so-called miracle medication because it caused his blood pressure to plummet, making everything even worse. The medication was primarily effective against proteinuria, when cats excrete too much protein in their urine. But, as we found out, Max didn't have any problems in that area. His urine should have been examined before the medication was prescribed. This would at least rule out the possibility of inflammation. And, the blood pressure should have been measured as well, since the medication affects it.

When his kidneys were examined using ultrasound, right away it became obvious that one was significantly smaller than the other. And, CKD-typical changes could already be observed on the kidney surface. During the ultrasound exam, his bladder was aspirated to access some sterile urine. I was very surprised that this wasn't a problem for Max at all. I stayed with him the whole time, caressed his head and talked to him. He was such a good boy. He sensed that there were people at work trying their best to help him.

The recommendation was simple: stop administering the Telmisartan medication, continue feeding the kidney diet as before, and in four weeks check the kidney function through blood levels. If he was stable then, the teeth would come next. Particularly in case of CKD, the teeth needed to be rehabilitated because inflammation of the gums is always bad for the kidney function. That made sense.

The vet explained the CKD process in detail to me, with subcutaneous infusions before, during and after the restoration of his teeth. These infusions provide water in order to optimally relieve the kidneys and immediately flush them again. "We can do a lot with CKD. But nothing can be done very quickly anymore," the vet said. She would be proven right.

Over the next four weeks, Max became increasingly fit. The homeopathic treatment continued, and that was OK with the veterinary clinic. So it could only be a plus.

When he was in much better shape at the next check-up, and the blood pressure and kidney function blood levels had returned to normal, we scheduled his dental restoration. The vet showed me where the tartar had built up and the current inflammations were located. She expected that lesions were underneath it. FORL (Feline odontoclastic resorptive lesion) is the name of the disease present in many cats. It develops from the inside out and thus often remains undetected, but causes much pain to the animals. Max's dental restoration was scheduled for September. He was to stabilize for a few more weeks. He would be under full anesthesia to receive a complete dental cleaning, dental X-rays, and then all bad teeth were to be extracted. In addition, he was to receive subcutaneous infusions before, during and after the procedure.

FLIX, DRY-FOOD JUNKIE

Flix came to us being a dry food junkie, there's no other way to describe it. Wet food was never his thing, but as soon as we put some pieces of dry food in his activity feeder, he became very excited. He trotted up to it and got busy locating and eating his food, visibly happy.

Flix also came to us carrying heavy baggage attached to his soul. He threw up quite often. We tried to find a pattern. When was it happening, in which situations, and what had he eaten before it? One pattern had to do with Cat Mum's absence. He didn't like that at all. Another pattern included eating too quickly, which at first happened a lot with his beloved dry food. A third pattern occurred when he shed his fur, which was easily treatable.

Both cats were used to me working at home, and not seeing Michael before Thursday evening and then over the weekend. Only once in a while do I have to go on a business trip, not more than 20% of the time. That allowed us all to get comfortable and find a mutual routine. Then I had to travel to the United States for four days, and for two of those days, we were able to have our lady neighbor be cat sitter, checking up on them twice a day. Flix threw up right away on the first day; then he recovered from the shock.

His latest blood tests, measured only a few weeks before he joined us, were very good. No signs at all of hidden inflammation in his body. We tried almost the entire first year to change his food habits. We ditched the dry food and used high-quality wet food instead. A few pieces of dry food were used only as treats, and he loved them twice as much when he got them. It took us about eight months to complete the process.

I can only tell everyone to make the effort and take the time to switch dry-food junkies to high-quality wet food. Since Flix preferred food with sauce, I looked for a high-quality organic food in its own juice, without any grain, which he found very tasty. Slowly, very slowly, in very small portions, I mixed the new food under the old food. At the animal shelter, he had received the same food as Max. At the same time, I gradually reduced the amount of dry food he had in his activity feeder. To adjust this very slowly is the most important step, and to relax the change a bit when it seems he balks at it, and stabilize the status quo before continuing.

Cats are habitual eaters. They will first reject everything they don't know from an early age. It is not at all true that cats know instinctively what is good for them. This might certainly be different with regard to wild cats, but not with domesticated cats. They have no choice. What humans give to them first after the kittens drank their mother's milk is to them what mother has "approved of," and will be accepted and eaten. Otherwise, cats would surely always opt for mice.

It was easier getting his vomiting under control when it was due to shedding his fur and spitting out thick fur balls with the food. This improved greatly with the help of malt paste and egg lecithin powder. Slowly we developed a routine to brush him. He wasn't used to that, but accepted it more and more.

We had his vomiting almost under control, but toward the end of the first year it became worse again. So, we decided to have him thoroughly examined, in the same veterinary clinic, by Max's vet. We had just stabilized Max after his first dental surgery. We used the quarterly check-up date for Max's CKD also to have Flix examined thoroughly.

It turned out that his kidney tests were OK, some values had only risen a little. But his inflammation levels had increased and the inflammation of his intestinal wall already showed in the blood analysis. The vet saw this as the main problem for his vomiting. It manifested itself either as diarrhea out the back or vomiting out the front. Flix got everything out through his mouth. He didn't have any diarrhea.

Due to the inflammation, his intestinal wall was already very thick. By introducing high-quality food, we were moving in the right direction. More about that in the chapter "Another Visit with the Vet."

Max's Dental Surgery,
Take One ...

In September, when Max had been with us nine months in his new and forever home, I took him to the veterinary clinic in the morning for his dental restoration. It meant that under full anesthesia, his teeth would be professionally cleaned and the tartar removed. Then his teeth would be examined with a dental X-ray device. This would detect the vicious dental disease called FORL[1] and a decision could be made whether and how many teeth had to be removed. These teeth would be extracted right after the exam. I was nervous. As a CKD patient, Max was to receive IV infusions before, during and after surgery.

At this point, I can wholeheartedly recommend having a dental X-ray taken before dental restoration. It is of no help to simply remove the tartar and not detect FORL. It would mean that the teeth look "good" on the surface, but the cat still experiences horrible pain. And just like in Max's case, the kidneys would continue to be damaged through this undetected

---

1. FORL = Feline odontoclastic resorptive lesions (also known as neck lesions, cervical line erosions, and cat cavities) are the most common dental problem in cats. Studies worldwide have shown incidence rates in cats presented for dental problems of up to 75%! Feline odontoclastic resorptive lesions (FORL) are painful. Clinical signs associated with FORL include anorexia, drooling, refusal to eat the hard portions of the diet, and overall malaise. The most common sign of pain in cats, however, is no sign at all. Source: https://vmcli.com/feline-dental-problems/

disease. FORL remains undetected for a long time because it develops from the inside of the teeth. It is an extremely painful autoimmune disease.

Unfortunately, you can't really detect it based on eating habits. In the cat community, I had heard repeatedly that cats with extremely damaged teeth were still eating "normally" without any outward signs of the disease.

Max had the talent to speak continuously in the car. He commented on the trip to the veterinary clinic in a very clear way and very directly; it moved me to tears; even before we arrived there.

He was checked in and hooked up to an IV to receive his infusions. We cuddled and I held him tight one last time. That was extremely difficult. I said right away that I would wait for the vet dentist. I didn't know her then, and under no circumstances would I just hand Max over to someone I didn't know. After all, his life depended on my decisions. No more and no less.

I had taken along my laptop. That way I could work for the next two hours. And then a little longer because there was an emergency and Max stayed hooked up to his IV for another hour. Then the vet dentist came to talk to me. We spoke for a short time and she explained everything again in detail. Right away, I had a good feeling. She would do a great job. I was so nervous because I suddenly realized that I was putting Max's life into her hands.

I heard myself ask her if I could see Max one more time. She gave me a quick look and understood completely what I was going through. She brought him and I took my Max in my arms and looked into his eyes. Big pupils were looking at me. "What are they doing to me here? How can you let this happen? I want to go home immediately. I am so afraid." I pressed him against me and told him that his teeth were going to be fixed and that I would pick him up again this evening and we would drive home together. Then I placed him back on the vet's arm and left the room. I couldn't hold back my tears any longer. All the pressure I had kept inside was breaking through. I drove home crying all the way. My Max! I hope I did the right thing. This was an emotional rollercoaster of the worst kind.

I sat next to the telephone, waiting for it to ring and hoping that the veterinary clinic would call me after the dental procedure. However, it rang right after I had stepped into the house. Oh my God, what had happened now? The vet explained to me that she had now cleaned and X-rayed Max's teeth. Quite to her surprise, Max's molars were healthy but two, actually three of his fangs had to be extracted, due to FORL. For this, she needed my approval. My poor Max. And what would the specialists recommend? The recommendation was clear: All teeth affected by FORL had to come out. Well, then we'll do exactly that.

So, I was back to waiting and sending a lot of energy to Max so he would get through this OK. The next call came when Max was already awake again, and still receiving infusions in order to flush his kidneys as best as possible after the anesthesia. I was able to pick him up in the evening, shortly after 6 pm.

When I arrived at the veterinary clinic, I first received instructions for the medication he needed for the next few days. It was a special pain medication belonging to the group of the opioids, for which I had to sign a special waiver, and an antibiotic to prevent potential infection. Then they brought Max to me with a cone around his neck. My poor Max, how long would he have to endure this? At least a week, the vet told me, to prevent the sutures in the front of his mouth from tearing; because there isn't a suitable material they could use to stitch it up a second time. I understood that. It was just that I knew my Max well. I didn't see him being able to comply with this for a whole week.

We got in the car and started to drive home. Being able to bring a beloved animal from the clinic back home is a special, wonderful feeling. First, I had done everything right to get the required veterinary treatment, in order to ensure my kitty's health. Now Max just had to be cared for at home to become healthy again. I was very glad to do that.

During the drive home, he first commented quite loudly on the day's events. These had been unnecessary and very annoying. What had I been thinking? And pulling fangs out of his mouth, that's really the worst; it was really diminishing his self-confidence as the boss cat. And, he believed he was doing really well anyway. So why all that? Of course, Max was high on his "drugs." Before going home, he had received three drops of the pain medication Buprenovet[1] so that he would feel better. The next dose was not to be administered until midnight.

---

1. Buprenovet, also called Buprenorphine in the US or Buprecare in other countries is a pain reliever in the opioid family, especially to treat post-operative pain. Max was given this drug because of his CKD, as it is more kidney-friendly than a conventional pain reliever. Depending on your country, it may fall under some kind of Narcotics Act, which is why you may only get the exact amount you need and you have to sign a corresponding document. More information: https://www.dvm360.com/view/feline-ckd-therapeutic-goals-do-not-throw-away-your-shot

As soon as we were home, Max marched with his cat cone out of the cat carrier. First, he went toward the litter box, bumping into everything to his left and right until he had "adjusted" himself again.

To my big surprise, he was hungry and first devoured a whole portion of food; and then another half portion. What a big relief! Eating wasn't going to be a problem for him.

Then I experimented. How could I best administer the antibiotic tablet? In little pieces stuffed into liverwurst, which we had purchased just for him. That seemed to be the right choice.

WHEN THE BOSS CAT
BECOMES THE PATIENT

Nothing worked as it had before. We learned that pretty quickly. Flix inspected and sniffed his companion Max quite critically. Then he distanced himself right away. No, he didn't want to have anything to do with this Max. The way he looked? And the way he smelled? Very suspicious.

Later this evening, when Max was seeking closeness, Flix even hissed at him. I hadn't expected that at all. A dear friend and cat expert, Mike from England, then provided me with the decisive hint: Max smells like the hospital and that doesn't bode well for Flix. "Go ahead and wash everything that was in the clinic," he said.

So I washed Max's little blanket. And gradually everything improved. Flix still didn't trust the situation. Why did his friend Max have an idiotic collar around his neck? But at least Flix didn't hiss at Max anymore. They slowly became closer again.

The next days were defined by Max's medication routine. Every eight hours I had to administer a few drops. At the same time, we were trying to return him to the normal eating routine and to integrate his kidney therapy.

Of course we wanted Max to feel as well as possible, and he should be able to go out wherever he wanted to go. It was early September; a sunny September. Max spent a lot of time on the balcony and enjoyed the sun.

Max recovered quickly from the surgery. It's amazing how much cats can endure. Imagine for a moment, how one of us humans would feel if we just had dental surgery during which all three canine teeth were removed.

During that time, I often thought of my wisdom tooth surgery, which I had to go through in my early twenties. All four teeth were pulled at the same time; because if you have only two taken out, you probably wouldn't voluntarily come back for the other two. For a whole week, I was basically out of commission. My face was swollen, my eyes almost shut; I was using ice packs continuously and taking very strong pain medication.

Despite giving as much care as Max needed, I still made an effort to spend enough time with Flix. Through his playful demeanor, Flix had become everybody's favorite. But, he also looked after Max, his friend and Boss Cat. It was always clear who decided about the direction of activities and how to proceed. However, it became increasingly difficult for Flix to continue moving about with certainty when it was clear that Max couldn't give direction, he had to first get healthy again. Flix, who loved to count on Max's leadership, had to make his decisions all by himself. Max needed his energy for himself.

Max could play the role of Boss Cat to a very limited degree, and that was a completely new situation for Flix—one that brought him a lot of heavy stress. After I had washed all the blankets and the smell of sickness had disappeared, things became easier. But, there was still the collar that Max wore around his neck. That irritated Flix very much.

Max didn't like it himself. On the third day, he actually found a solution to get rid of it. The wooden panels that we had on the balcony and loggia with many spaces in between them were ideal for removing the collar. He only had to squeeze the collar in one of these spaces and try to move it a bit. And then, off it was, that annoying thing. The first time I discovered the collar missing, I put it back around his neck. That didn't last too long. Max knew how to get rid of it and had more patience than I did.

So I didn't put the collar on again. Of course, I made it very clear to him that he was not allowed to try and gnaw on the sutures in his mouth. He seemed to be aware of that. He never tried anything with the sutures. What an awesome, wise cat!

Everything healed up very well, and after three days, he didn't want any more pain medicine. After ten days we had a follow-up appointment at the veterinary clinic. The vet was happy with the healing progress, and

Max's kidney test levels were back to where they were before the surgery. We were told to return for a check-up in December, a good sign. Max had seen enough of vets and clinics. When the dentist who had taken him into her heart looked into his face, she only said to me, "… Max is thinking, oh … that person again." She was laughing. She understood him well.

Soon Max was his usual self again, and Flix was happy about it. By now, fall was approaching. The relationship between the two cats had normalized. Max was the Boss Cat again in the house, and sat on top of the cat tree like a king. Flix felt more secure, and sat on "his" cat tree with a view. Both enjoyed their life.

First Experiences with Animal Communication

Ever since we've known Flix, he always acted fearful and often overly careful. He would be lying somewhere and when we walked by him, he would jump up and leave. No exception. From the very beginning, we had spoken with him with calm and loving voices to build up his trust, which he had apparently lost. It was very obvious that one or more experiences had caused great damage to his soul.

Even when we visited him at the animal shelter in the back part of the cat dwelling, we noticed he tried to remain undetected and avoided being touched. At first, he would allow one of us to approach him only very carefully and with a quiet voice.

However, Flix also showed that he would like to trust someone again, that he wanted to allow closeness and love. But, too many bad experiences and fears from his previous life seemed to block this ability. We could read it all in his eyes. He was a very sensitive soul, burdened by a profound sadness. But, a soul that was also ready to put his trust in someone again, to open up again, when the right conditions were met. And, he was definitely looking for these conditions. Although he often ran off, he always came back to us. That's when he wanted to be stroked and held. In the beginning, he never stayed long. In the blink of an eye, he had taken off again and disappeared.

It was quite clear that he had attached himself to Max. Max made the decisions. When Max defined a place as safe, then Flix used it as well. When

Max okayed guests, Flix, in due time, also accepted them. Max had already taken him under his wings at the animal shelter; we could easily see it. Max protected Flix and made sure that both of them could move from the animal shelter to their forever home.

When strangers visited, Flix scooted and jumped onto the top of the cabinet to observe everything from a safe distance, from above. Only people very experienced with cats, like our dear friend Wally, were able to get close without him retreating any further on the cabinet. Astoundingly, he even let her touch him, but only very gentle petting and not too much. But, he allowed no holding at all. You can never be careful enough.

I really wanted to get a better understanding of what he had gone through in his life before he came to us. He was already 15 years old, if this age estimate by the shelter was correct. Whatever his true age was, he was no youngster for sure.

Our cat sitter, who took care of both of them when I had to travel, had really loved Flix from the first day. She was a trained animal caretaker, and had no problems with giving them their medication. She knew how to play with them, especially with Flix. She felt he was a cat that you would want to carry around the whole day. Want? Sure; but not as far as Flix was concerned. If there was one thing he hated, it was the mere attempt by a human to pick him up, let alone carry him around. No, that wasn't possible. Not under any circumstances.

She was allowed to give him treats from the first day on, but touching? "No, we are not that familiar with each other," said Flix. That took a long time. The cat sitter was happy about every small step forward, which showed that Flix trusted her a little bit more. I was so happy about the notes she wrote, such as: "Flix and I are becoming better friends every day!"

How could we get a better understanding of what Flix experienced and what was troubling him? Animal communication was the answer. As it often happens in life, the universe is very involved when our intention is clear and honest. My first contact for communicating with animals was absolutely the right one. When I think back on it now, what we were able to achieve with Sylvia's help, I am tremendously grateful. Through her work, she achieved a lot of wonderful things for both cats and played a decisive part in securing their happiness.

Our desire to find out what had happened in both of their pasts, what made them the way they were, was the entry into a wonderful world of animal communication. I was researching the soul world of animals, conversations with animals, and people who offered to teach about it. Then, I selected someone simply based on my feeling. That's how I found Sylvia's Internet presence. I contacted her and asked her to talk to Flix. I told her I wanted to get more information about his past, about the things he experienced, so that we could best help reduce his anxieties. All she needed for that was a picture of Flix that showed his eyes clearly, and a few questions that we wanted to ask him. The "animal conversation" would be conducted long distance and she would then send me her notes. Super. So I quickly wired the financial energy (her fee), selected a few pictures, and emailed them to her together with the questions I had. Then we waited in eager anticipation of what Flix would have to say.

In early September, a few days before Max's dental surgery, the notes of the conversation arrived:

Dear Tamara,

Now here is what Flix communicated to me:

Body feelings:

I feel Flix's lower back, a blockage in the sacroiliac joint, which can be felt in the left hip. I can feel these continuously, as well as the left knee, the upper thigh over the knee, on the outside and the shin bone up front and on the side. The ankle joint is also tingling a bit (from an old injury). I feel pressure and burning on the inside in the center of the belly area (stomach? pancreas?) and a blockage in the middle of the thoracic spine.

Flix can't see clearly, everything is a bit blurred. I sense pressure over the eyes and a bit of "wooziness" in the head. I can sense pressure in the ears (I am not sure whether or not he hears well. Sounds seem "quieter," they seem to be farther away and muffled?) The jaw joints are tense and I sense the teeth are sensitive and the gums are burning a little, all of them, but more in the front of the mouth. In the chest area, I sense a feeling of tightness all around (heart?) and he doesn't take deep breaths (this could be caused by the blockage in the thoracic spine).

General observations:

He carries a deep sadness inside, a baggage he's been carrying from his previous life. Flix is a really sweet, calm, very gentle and sensitive soul. He is immensely grateful for what he has now, this home, this feeling of security, this love, this chance ... of this life. Because he has seen a lot and also experienced many disappointing encounters with humans. (I have tears in my eyes as he is telling me that ... There is so much gratitude and peace in him; the peace he has finally found now. He's showing me a red, very soft, cuddly material ... a sweater or a blanket that he snuggles up with and I feel a strong love in his heart.) Flix needs times when he retreats into his cave and he is happy there, feels safe and secure.

Past:

Retreating into a cave is something he knows as protection from his earlier life. Flix shows me a piece of cardboard box. There is a cardboard box somewhere and it is cold. Someone has put a blanket inside. He is in a barn, or a car port which is open in the front. The box is sitting somewhat higher, on a table? Lots of miscellaneous stuff, utensils, furniture? It's all just sitting there, and it's old and dusty. It's a hideout for him, because it is very uncomfortable outside. It's a place to sleep. Flix shows me various pictures from his past and I deduce that he went through several stations of life. He shows me a picture in which he looks up to a window of an older building where several families live, again and again. The entrance door is made of glass and metal and remains closed. The curtains aren't moving. He meows. Softly. He waits a long time there, does it again and again, for weeks. That's where his sadness comes from. There was a human living there who didn't want him anymore, who left him, or maybe died? Moved away? He shows me a woman in a very endearing way. She is a little older, and alone. She was his caretaker. He doesn't know where she is, she didn't say goodbye. Just like that. This disappointment hit him hard. Then an odyssey began when he didn't have a home anymore. He showed me a street that he crosses, avoiding a car just in the nick of time.

He shows me the carport that he used as a shelter, but he didn't find a home. I feel that it is cold. I see milk being poured onto an old porcelain dish with a flower pattern ... I see humans but they have no faces. I see cats that are fat and want to fight, want to chase him from their territory. I sense uncertainty and more and more sadness. Flix has given up on himself, only tries to survive, struggles along, and

love and security are missing ... he wanted to go home. He wanted
it so much. Then he was at the animal shelter but felt hopeless ...
Who would want an old tomcat, a member of the lost ones of whom
there are so many? And then YOU came along ... a ray of light in the
dark. Even today, he can't believe his luck ...

"I love you so much and thank both of you for everything!"

Now:

Yes, Flix enjoys the hands that caress, the closeness, the security,
and the love, very much! He likes your voice! And your laughter!
Often, his happiness could be overflowing and he doesn't know what
to do with all his wonderful feelings and he runs around and plays
like crazy to show his happiness and to make you laugh. He is simply
extraordinarily thankful and happy, and feels incredibly comfortable
at your home!!! Why does he look at you so intensely ... Because he
shares a deep connection with you ... because he recognizes something in you, sees something in your soul that is a part of himself. A
similarity, a desire, something lost a long time ago ... he knows that
this is what brought you together and he hopes to have enough time
left to be together and to heal.

Thank you Flix!

Dear Tamara. I look forward to hearing from you!

Heartfelt Greetings

Sylvia

Wow! Very moving, very stirring. I was deeply touched and cried many
tears. I read his conversation with Sylvia over and over again. My little Flix!
Everything made more sense now, it had become a story. Flix's story. The
heavy burden on his soul when he came to us made a lot of sense now.

The conversation itself was changing Flix. He became much more open.
He seemed very relieved having been able to trust someone with all these experiences. Now, based on the new knowledge from the conversation, we needed to
engage with him in a different way that was more specific regarding his needs.

Once in a while, instead of running off he now kept lying down when
one of us walked past him. Very slowly, his behavior was changing. He
became more relaxed, understood more and more that he was in a place he
can call home, where nothing bad would ever happen to him.

He realized that his humans loved him immensely. And, because love is the strongest energy we have, it is energy capable of true miracles, capable of real changes. From that point on, and little by little, his trust was growing again.

Sunny Places and Raspberry Cats

A lofty apartment on the fourth and fifth floor with a loggia and balcony is bright and sunny! Enough sunshine for two cats hungry for sunshine—or so one would think.

But this was apparently not the case. The sun shone in the morning on the loggia. During spring and summer, when the weather was nice, I opened the door for them in the morning, so they could get out and lie down for a sunbath. As I said, there was plenty of room for both of them.

But the "tomcat" pecking order came into play here. It happened again and again that Max drove Flix away from Flix's sunny spot to lie down exactly there instead. Flix then, most of the time, just took off rather perturbed. Only later, he learned to put his paw down and looked for another spot. I never really found out what went on between the two of them, because there were also moments when they would be lying in the sun, all relaxed and not far away from each other.

From noon and through the afternoon, the sun had moved to the other side of the building, onto the balcony. So, locations had to be switched. Max loved to simply walk around on the balcony, inspect all flower pots, and finally lie down in the sun.

During the first summer, Flix developed into what I call a "raspberry cat." He ate almost all the raspberries that we had been growing. I caught him more than once taking his time inspecting the raspberries, stretching and stretching, and then finally reaching and eating them. I asked myself for a long time what he was lacking that he acquired a liking for raspberries.

It must have been the potassium. Later, when his blood screening showed a very low potassium level, he received dietary supplements to prevent potential damage to his heart.

After this first summer, he never again was interested in our raspberries. The potassium obviously found a different way into his body.

CAT NETS

The two of them moved into their new home in January. So enough time was left until spring to familiarize ourselves with the topic of cat nets.

It became clear over the first weeks that we had to learn about cat nets. Because during his explorations, Max found out that he could easily crawl through the balcony railing and climb onto the roof of the building, which wasn't safe at all. We were on the fourth floor!

At first, both cats were never alone on the balcony. Max was very eager to explore all kinds of things. After his first intended roof excursion, I suspected his intentions and made sure he never got a chance to do this. There was no question about it, the balcony needed a cat net if we all wanted to enjoy it in peace, and give both cats the freedom to come out on the balcony and go back inside on their own.

Since our balcony was the highest one, simple solutions like tying the net to a neighboring balcony weren't possible. We needed some experts. I quickly made a few acquaintances in the local cat group, with whom we were able to discuss the topic of cat nets.

There were a lot of fans of "do-it-yourself." We took a look at some of these examples. It wasn't going to be that easy in our case. So, we were looking for a professional cat net builder and found one. He was also the only one who gave us a concrete quote based on our plans.

Soon after that, two craftsmen came to our apartment with the new cat net and installed it. That was done very quickly. It looked very stable and good, very professional. The two workers looked at Max and Flix who were standing nearby, being a bit shy. They seemed to be asking "What are these men doing here?" When the men found out that the cats had come from the animal shelter, they had to smile. "Really? Just came from the shelter and already getting such a fine net?"

They also let us know if one of the cats started gnawing on the net or tried to climb up it, we should stop the cat immediately. Because yes, cats can ruin everything. Yes, of course. Only, our two little tigers had never damaged anything before.

We leave the loggia unsecured to this day. Max tried once to jump from the kitchen window sill onto to the loggia railing. I told him in no uncertain terms that he wasn't allowed to do that. He never tried it again. Flix never tried it at all.

AT THE TABLE WITH MAX

No one could possibly miss that Max was an extraordinarily wise cat. And, he acted that way too. Different. He wanted to participate in eating at the table. His way.

During the first few months, he used to jump in my lap and kept me company when I was eating. When Michael joined us on the weekend, he took the opportunity and did the same with his Cat Dad. Max really enjoyed these moments; one could sense how he just soaked up all the love.

In the summer when we usually ate outside, he was mostly with us too.

It went without saying that he climbed onto "his" lawn chair on the balcony when I was sitting there in the evenings. He resided at the table like a king and watched his Cat Mum. Just being Sir Max. And we conversed.

In the summertime, the lawn chair increasingly became his relaxation and retreating spot. With a light breeze and a comfortable chair, his recovery wasn't going to be a problem at all.

He looked quite natural on his throne. My dear friend Fiona once described him as "like an emperor." He acted as if he had sat there forever, ruling the world from the balcony on the fourth floor.

When we both wanted to sit out there on the weekends, Max was often quicker than Michael and was already occupying his (!) seat. But Cat Dad also wanted to sit somewhere. So what did the world's best Cat Dad do?

Simply said: "Enjoy your life, Max," pulled up a third lawn chair, and then Max on his chair was pushed in the middle between us.

Sometimes Max would also inspect the food. Since everything except cat food is vegan in our house, we often smiled when Max eyed our food and even sniffed it once in a while. In most cases, he wasn't interested in continuing these tasting sessions. How fortunate for all participants!

However, he put on a surprised look the first time he saw a green smoothie. "Unbelievable what crazy stuff humans ingest," he seemed to think, and then returned to enjoying his morning sunbath.

Whenever he had surgery and needed to recuperate, one of his favorite spots was the balcony and "his" lawn chair. He would sit there for hours in the afternoon, watch the sun move, and just relax. He seemed to be far, far away in his cat world!

When Max declared the balcony to be secure, Flix also felt safe and came out with him. But, Flix was always looking for a spot close to the wall of the house, not anywhere near the railing. He felt much safer on the loggia. Especially without Max.

KING OF THE STRAYS

Shortly after Max's first dental restoration, when I was trying to deal with Flix's communication, I remained a little curious regarding Max. What had Max's life been like? What was burdening his soul? So, I asked Sylvia to have a talk with Max as well. A few weeks after the surgery, he could certainly find an open spot in his calendar in order to talk to Sylvia.

Max's communication has touched me deeply as well. Here are a few excerpts from Sylvia's conversation with Max:

Yes, the surgery has damaged his self-confidence a bit, he told me because he's now got a lisp :-) and he still has a strange feeling in his mouth. Dumb!

Past: What he experienced? *"Well ... quite a lot!"* (He shows me a picture while we talk, showing him "strutting" through high grass ... So, in order not to get dirty and wet. That is sweet.) *"I spent a lot of time outside. Sometimes it wasn't easy. But I was the king of the strays!"* (Yes, that's exactly what he said.) *"I was responsible for many other cats, I had a job. I protected them all and watched out for them. Some were sick or simply disappeared. Sometimes I still think back on it."* Max shows me pictures ... a big farm with machines and barns and buildings.

"When I was small, I was ill. I saw a tunnel and the light; wanted to go home because it's warm and easy there. But there was a woman with a good heart and a gentle voice. She held me, took me back and that's how I became Max again." (He grins)

Max never had a real home and he hates disorder. Everything must be in its place, now when he's doing well and feels so comfortable and at home. He enjoys it so much and is so grateful for it!!! That's why he can hardly relax and always has to look whether or not everything is still in its place or has suddenly disappeared. So that the soft carpet, the upholstery on the chair, all these wonderful amenities which he loves so much don't suddenly disappear. And he wakes up and it turns out that everything was just a dream.

But he still has to manage everything, must take it in his paws and can never be sure of anything or simply lean back and relax (sometimes, atop the cat tree, it really works; then he is on cloud nine :-) and yes, in his dreams, he is even cooler than in real life :-) and trust things are going to be fine.

How did he meet Flix I want to know? *"Well, there was a car that picked him up,"* he tells me. And then he was at the animal shelter. And there was Flix. And he felt sorry for Flix who was so sad and something in him reminded him of this sadness. It touched his soul and he felt responsible and started to protect him the way he always protected everyone. *"This seems to be my task,"* he said, blinking his eyes. *"I just feel it within me. And that's how it'll always be. We are all connected."* He looks into the distance, and I sense that I have an old soul in front of me which had already lived many times and carries wisdom that transcends a normal cat life.

"Yes", he says, *"I have to protect them. I found them; like they found me. It was just like it was with Flix. I had a feeling inside. It was supposed to be like that. I want them to be happy. That they don't worry so much about things that aren't worth worrying about. Life often provides miracles; one must only recognize them and take advantage of the opportunity. And always be alert. :-) The trust thing I still have to learn. Tell them please that I love them very much. And I like it when the floor is warm* (in the bathroom?) *and I just like everything the way it is. THANK YOU!!!!"*

———————

When I read how he met Flix and took care of him right away because he was so sad, it made me tear up and it still does, again and again; my Max, such a brave hero; a savior, always ready to help; feeling responsible to take charge, to be there for others; perfect feline leadership.

What a wonderful soul ... my Max!

And yes, the dental restoration had hurt his feline self-confidence quite a bit. He didn't want to talk more about it. Well yes, I can imagine. But there was no alternative for it. The broken teeth would have continued to damage his kidneys and caused him even more pain.

ANOTHER VISIT WITH THE VET

S hortly before Christmas, we took both of them to the vet. Max was due for his kidney check-up with geriatric blood panel. And, we also wanted a geriatric blood panel done for Flix and wanted to have him examined because his vomiting returned at times. We didn't think this could be caused simply by any stress he was feeling.

Max provided a blood sample and allowed his blood pressure to be taken. He seemed to disregard most of the action, but commented on it with the occasional hiss in the vet's direction. The vet only said: "Max was such a good boy when he came here for the first time and his blood pressure was way too low." Was—definitely the operative word. He obviously didn't have that problem anymore. His blood pressure now was close to the upper tolerance limit, but didn't need to be treated as of now. And, of course, he was back in his Max prime energy.

Unfortunately, his creatinine level had hardly gone down, although we had hoped it would after the extraction of his bad teeth. But it hadn't gone up either, which was a positive development. "Stable in a bad way" said the vet tersely and to the point. She also recommended extraction of the upper molars in the near future because they had become worse just over the last few months.

Even I could recognize that. The gums were slightly inflamed and tartar had built back up in record time. However, Max didn't seem to feel any pain, so we planned to have the next surgery in the spring to have enough time between the surgeries. My poor Max, another dental surgery very soon. Well, it couldn't be avoided. Because it would keep his kidneys working longer and allow him a more comfortable life, we just had to have it done.

Then it was Flix's turn. He was so nervous that his paws turned bright red. He was very tense but endured the exam and blood draw patiently. After the vet felt his abdomen, an ultrasound exam was performed. I remained close to his head and stroked him and talked to him the whole time. He was able to relax for a few moments, but tensed up right away. That didn't make the ultrasound exam any easier or shorter.

His intestinal wall was too thick due to inflammation. The size of his kidneys had decreased and they had changed slightly on the surface, but were in much better shape than Max's. The vet was planning to contact us as soon as the blood results were available.

Then Flix had reached the end of his patience; he was very stressed and peed. I put him on his blanket and lifted him in my arm and cuddled him. Even though he still didn't like to be picked up, for the moment, Cat Mum's arm seemed to be the safest place. He hid right away and became almost invisible in the crook of my arm.

We needed to return home quickly, to the calm and secure environment. The blood results arrived a few days later with recommendations for his therapy.

But first, Christmas was almost here. It was the first for both of them in their new forever home; and the first one for us with our wonderful cats.

STRESS ON NEW YEAR'S EVE

We had the foresight not to plan anything for our first New Year's Eve with the two of them. We planned to stay at home and spend the time with our cats. We had no idea yet how they would react to all the firecracker noise.

The stress began a few days earlier. My mother-in-law was visiting and a few days before New Year's Eve, we wanted to go out to a restaurant together. A wonderful idea, we thought. Unfortunately, on that day—three days before New Year's Eve—people were already setting off firecrackers like crazy. Flix was quite nervous. You could see the uneasiness in his eyes; a look of fear returned. He was pacing around, very tense; Max, at least outwardly, didn't seem to mind anything that was going on.

When we got ready to go, Flix had suddenly disappeared. We couldn't find him in any of his hiding places. You can feel quite silly when you can't find an indoor cat. But everyone who has cats knows that this is part of the program.

So we went up, then down, up again, down again, searched all the usual places, including the storage closet and under the bed. No luck. We checked all closets and cabinets. I would never leave without knowing where Flix was or how he was doing.

Suddenly, I got an idea and looked under the dresser in the hallway. He had never crawled under there, but my intuition guided me to look there.

And there he was, trembling in fear. Under the dresser, although we didn't really understand how he had been able to even get under there.

Michael and my mother-in-law went to the restaurant and I stayed with Flix and Max. There was no way I was going to leave Flix home alone when he was so scared.

We lifted the dresser up a little with a few paperback books so he was able to crawl out without twisting his hips or some other part of his body. Later this evening he came back out and fled into my lap. He felt secure there. I felt how tense and nervous he was all over.

The same happened for several evenings, including New Year's Eve. Flix was completely exhausted. Max kept walking with majestic movements through Flix's territory and tried, more than usually, to give off strength and control to calm his friend Flix down.

The following year, everything became a little less tense at this occasion. Flix had built up much more trust and was able to manage his fears better. The stress that happened the following year began shortly after New Year's Eve.

Flix's Therapy:
Alternatives Are Needed

When Flix's blood test results arrived and the diagnosis was completed, the vet called me. Inflammation in the bowel (gastroenteritis) which had already been detected through the ultrasound, could also be seen in the blood test. The inflammation and kidney test levels were slightly higher. We needed to definitely keep an eye on that. But first, his gastroenteritis had to be brought under control.

A short, relatively high-dose cortisone therapy was recommended to me. If that didn't help, another visit to the vet would be required. At that point in time, I had not familiarized myself with this topic. So, I went ahead and accepted the recommendation, received the Prednisolone for him and we started the therapy. That should work. So I thought.

Flix had a completely different idea about his therapy. He rejected the cortisone outright. I first put it in treats and liverwurst. Both of these ruses worked great with Max, but failed miserably with Flix. He took apart the treat or liverwurst piece that I had worked hard to assemble, revealed the tablet and looked at me accusingly: "Do you want to poison me?"

OK. This wasn't going to work. Hiding the pills in food, no matter how well I tried, was doomed from the start. That was my first attempt. So I thought about other, smarter ways to get it done.

I found empty capsules in different sizes and tablet dispensers for cats. So I ordered these utensils. Well, what can I say? Flix remained steadfast, very steadfast. He just didn't want to take this medication at all.

Everyone who has cats experiences these situations. You finally have the tablet in the empty capsule, and somehow you're able to put your cat between your legs and, with the tablet dispenser, successfully place the tablet into the cat's mouth. I breathed a sigh of relief and praised Flix for his good attitude.

And then, a moment later, I hear him choke and wham, the tablet was lying next to me on the sofa, behind the sofa, under the table, or was vomited directly in front of my feet. Flix was very good at all these variations.

OK, I do listen to my little tigers; I want to know what they think. The message was utterly clear: "Whatever you are trying to do, I am not going to take the pills."

We needed to find other ways. I spent most of the next days researching. What would be an alternative method for treating gastroenteritis, which to me meant without cortisone.

Because of Max's CKD, I had already joined a Facebook group on that subject. Now, I looked for a group for Flix's problem and found one. Unfortunately, the members were rather narrow-minded and condemned everything that wasn't related to academic medicine. Well, that wasn't helpful at this point.

I never condemned academic medicine and I won't do it in the future. It certainly has its purpose. But, like all other theories and approaches, it doesn't have the answers for all questions. I am not following any ideology; I am rather focused on integrating and combining different approaches as required. My first goal was always to find the best therapy for the situation at hand. And for that, the patient is the most important factor. And, Flix expressed himself very clearly.

I would learn later that all living beings possess a specific energy frequency. It can decrease when many blockages are present in the energy field, or it can increase when these blockages are cleared. The medication, which affects the patient in specific situations, must suit the patient's energy frequency. In this case, it could simply not be achieved with Prednisolone. Animals sense that instinctively.

At last, I found a solution with TCM, Traditional Chinese Medicine. I found a mix of herbs for cats in tablet form, called Gastro, which addressed exactly what Flix had. So I ordered it for him.

You won't believe it, but these tablets were exactly right for him in this situation. He took them without a problem, mixed in with his food and later in cat cream. No problem. And his condition improved. He stopped vomiting almost completely.

HAY CATS

What? An indoor cat and hay? How is this going to work? Well, I only needed encouragement from my good friend from Munich, Beate, who brought with her real Bavarian hay for both of them. She knew from her own experience how much cats love to roll around in hay. So, she decided that Max and Flix also needed hay.

When the high-quality Bavarian hay arrived, I re-designated a cardboard box as hay box. Then, I was eager to find out how the two boys would react to the hay.

And wouldn't you know! They had a blast with their hay. In the middle of the living room, mind you!

They tried out many things. First, Max, being the Boss Cat, had to inspect the hay. It met all his tough criteria. So he jumped into the box and lay down in the hay. Then Flix could also dare come closer and take a whiff. But, Max would not allow him to get in the box at the same time.

They chased each other into and out of the box. They were absolutely delighted. During the first year, then during the second year, and then they stopped. When Flix was alone for a few months in 2017, he wasn't interested in the hay anymore. And later, Howy didn't really take to it either. The hay period just faded out.

It was a lot of fun, which had a lot to do with Max. He most certainly remembered his time at the farm. He often spent many hours sleeping peacefully in the hay.

Flix, judging from his paws, had never been much of a fan of the outdoors, avoiding it except for the time he ended up in the streets.

DENTAL SURGERY, TAKE 2

We had known for a few months now that Max needed another dental surgery. When we had his CKD checked again in April, he appeared to be physically stable, but his kidney test levels had worsened slightly. So, we scheduled the surgery for the end of May. Before that, our vet wanted to see Max one more time.

The weeks before the surgery were very busy. I had my Spiritual Leadership Seminar in Scotland. As always, I had a hard time leaving my two beloved cats at home, even for just a few days. They were taken care of perfectly, two days by our cat sitter, and Michael worked the rest of the week at home. Nevertheless, at the airport, I found myself crying again.

As soon as I returned, Max and I were absolutely happy! You couldn't tell which of us was happier.

Regarding his CKD diagnosis, I once more consulted the CKD group on Facebook to prepare him as well as possible for the surgery. I pulled out all the stops to achieve that goal.

In addition to his combination of homeopathy (SUC) therapy, Max also received another homeopathic medication to strengthen his kidney function. At the same time, he was given another medication to strengthen his liver function. And, absolutely new, Cordyceps sinensis, a rare medicinal mushroom, which was also supposed to stimulate kidney function. When I was researching intestinal problems that plagued Flix, I had also looked for other options for Max's kidneys.

This is how I came upon the healing mushrooms, at a research institute that included an online shop with everything of organic quality; and telephone consultation which I took advantage of right away. I introduced my two little tigers and received very sound advice for both of them from the animal health practitioner at the institute. Because Flix had a good supply of his TCM tablets, I didn't want to change anything that very moment. So, it was Max who benefited from the medicinal mushrooms, Cordyceps sinensis. I learned how to carefully sneak it in, using small amounts to avoid any initial negative reactions. Max accepted the mushroom powder with a little bit of cat cream, or in his food, without any complaints. No problem, he liked his mushroom powder and it benefited him greatly.

We pursued a full program to prepare Max as best as we could for surgery. Because he was, as he pointed out himself, not a very young cat anymore.

The pre-surgery appointment at the vet caused no stress at all. She liked Max a lot and no needles were required this time. She wanted to get familiar with his condition and determine what exactly needed to be done during the dental restoration. It was apparent that tartar was building up rapidly. Because X-rays of his teeth from last September had not revealed any FORL of his molars, she was very interested to see in what shape his teeth would be this time around.

She explained to me the relationship between teeth and kidneys. Not only did dental diseases put strain on the kidneys, but conversely, the CKD caused an altered composition of his saliva which then attacked the teeth and the periodontium. Because the salivary glands are, in the case of cats, located on the upper jaw, the upper molars will be the first teeth to be affected.

We agreed that she would extract all teeth that needed to be extracted. I trusted her judgment, and didn't think it was necessary for her to call me once Max was already under anesthesia. She said, quite rightly, that considering Max's advanced age and his rather high creatinine levels, it was better not to do anesthesia a third time.

In late May, I took Max to the veterinary clinic for his surgery. As always, Max had a lot to say during the drive there. When we arrived, he became quiet at once and looked at me. His vet who had cared for him all the other times at the clinic took him from me. As always, I pressed him against my body and assured him that taking out his sick teeth was the right thing to do; that way they wouldn't cause him pain anymore. Then he was hooked up to an IV and I drove back home. Not as emotional as last time, but still very affected. What else did my beloved soul cat have to endure? Now that he had finally found a loving home, CKD attacked him with a vengeance. I really wished that the last years of his life would have been much more peaceful.

Just as I did last time, I tried to work at home while he was away. I wasn't very successful. My thoughts and feelings were with Max at the veterinary clinic. I received the expected phone call in the afternoon. The vet told me that all molars had to be extracted. So the internists had been accurate. She said she was really surprised that the condition of the teeth and the periodontium had worsened so much over the last nine months. She also told me that the creatinine level was at 4.9 mg/dl[1] before the surgery. That means it was high time to extract the teeth. Only six weeks earlier, the level had been 4.5. I know of other cases where such high creatinine levels had led to conditions that were so bad, that often surgery could not be done anymore.

I was able to pick Max up in the evening. This time he didn't have to wear a collar around his neck. That was a great relief. Just like last time, he was prescribed an opioid, a pain medication which he was supposed to take every eight hours, as well as an antibiotic for the next five days to prevent any kind of infection.

As soon as he arrived at home, Max really had to use the litter box. After that, he devoured a portion of food with a healthy appetite. Flix wasn't as skeptical this time around. Max didn't wear a cat cone, so that was good. Soon I washed Max's little blanket we had taken to the clinic to get rid of the hospital smell.

The next few days were spent taking really good care of Max. Again, we had to try every trick in the book to get him to take the antibiotic tablets and the opioid. Crushing the tablets and packing them in the liverwurst didn't always work. Sometimes it worked better to cut the tablets up in little pieces and hide them completely in the liverwurst. With the pain medication, we

---

1. In the US, creatinine is measured in mg/dl. Internationally, you may find the creatinine levels measured in μmol/L. This page provides a great overview: http://felinecrf.org/diagnosis _test_ranges_factors.htm#normal_ranges_blood_urine

went through the same experience as last time. After three days, he refused to take it. I trusted his decision.

A lot of time and effort went into Max's follow-up care, to make his recovery as easy for him as possible. It was now almost June, and Max enjoyed the morning hours on the loggia in the sun and afternoon sun on the balcony.

Max again recovered from the surgery surprisingly well. The appointment ten days later was very successful. The vet was happy with her work and the kidney test levels had already improved compared to before the surgery. It was time to breathe another sigh of relief. For his kidneys, I stayed with the combination of homeopathy (SUC) and Cordyceps sinensis healing mushrooms.

Now we were ready for summer, and Max would hopefully be able to spend the rest of his days without any medical procedures.

FLIX'S DEPRESSIVE PHASE

I remember exactly the day in early May when I had to visit the vet with Max to discuss his upcoming dental surgery. I didn't plan to take Flix along—that would have been his worst fear—but from one moment to the next, he had disappeared. I knew he couldn't have just "evaporated," he had to be somewhere. But, he wanted to make sure that he couldn't be found.

When I came back home with Max, he was still nowhere to be found. I searched the entire apartment, both floors and still couldn't find him anywhere. Until I had the idea to look in the storage closet. There he lay, rolled up on my yoga blanket. I sat down next to him, talked to him, stroked him and told him that everything was good, that he wasn't supposed to come with us anyway, and that Max was doing fine. Everything was good, but Flix wanted to stay in the closet. Only in the evening, when I sat down next to him again and caressed him, was he ready to come out. After that, for the next couple of days, everything pretty much went its normal way.

It was May and we had beautiful, sunny days. Both cats could again enjoy the sun, either on the loggia or the balcony. But Flix, all of a sudden, preferred being in the dark storage closet. I kept visiting him there and tried to get him out. However, he preferred to remain in the closet by himself.

In late May, it was almost time for Max's dental surgery. I explained to Flix beforehand that Max was going to have this surgery and he, Flix, could of course stay at home and didn't have to come along to the vet. I also told him that Max now needed a lot of energy, especially to recover from the surgery. Therefore, Max wouldn't be able to take care of him the way he usually does.

On the day of the dental surgery, we had the same problem again. As soon as Flix noticed that this was the day of all days, he dashed off to the closet. He didn't come back out until it was evening and Max was back home. He sniffed him intensely, to make absolutely sure that "his" Max had returned in good condition. "Well, we just dodged a bullet there, he's back again" is what I sensed from Flix.

But, Flix's behavior didn't return to normal. When we were later hit by several storms with hail, thunder, and lightning, he went immediately back into the storage closet. He only came back out in the late evening. Max wasn't bothered at all by the same storm. He continued lying on his red carpet, letting nothing spoil his day. The following two weeks brought similar thunderstorms.

Every time, Flix became very insecure and fled into the storage closet.

Flix was easily scared again and overly fearful. Not like in the beginning, when he took off as soon as someone came too close to him. Now, he didn't run away from us anymore. On the contrary, he had built up a lot of trust. It seemed like he was instead running from something unknown. He seemed triggered by certain situations.

One evening, when he was climbing out of the storage closet, I heard him scream. A scream that shook me to the core. Flix had never screamed before. Never had he spoken with such a powerful voice. He seemed to be in awful pain. He stood on the stairs and held his right front leg in the air. My first thought was: "He sprained his leg." He came hobbling down the stairs on three legs.

Of course he didn't want to be touched and hid in a corner instead. I usually make quick decisions in such situations, switching to "autopilot" so-to-speak. Was he in pain? Obviously. Could I handle this all by myself? Probably not. Did I need Flix's help instead? Yes. So I called the Hofheim Veterinary Clinic, they said "Of course, bring him by, emergency service is ready."

Flix sensed right away that he was going to be put in the carrier and hobbled back upstairs. In the bedroom, he lay down on the bed and stayed there, completely exhausted. At last, I could get close to him. I could assure him that all I wanted was to help him; that we had to find out what was going on with his leg and why he couldn't put it down anymore. He finally relaxed, he let me stroke him and calm him down. I was able to touch his little leg. It didn't feel swollen, but he pulled it back right away. Touching it was clearly painful for him. Taking him to the veterinary clinic right away was the correct decision.

He even let me carry him on my arm, which was a rare event, and I was able to put him in the transport box. When he realized how serious the situation was, he escaped one more time. On three legs! I had to use a lot of convincing power, and needed to be resolute picking him up and "packing him up" one more time. Finally we were ready to drive off.

On the way to the clinic he sat next to me in his box, letting me know what he thought quite loudly, which was very atypical for him. Nevertheless, it seemed like he sat there with a sense of pride because he was the center of attention. Something dawned on me ... Then he became quiet and lay down.

We had just arrived at the clinic and right away it was our turn. The vet on duty first listened to me telling him what happened, and looked at Flix's previous record. Then I opened the cat carrier to take Flix out. I was told to put him on the floor right away so we could see how he walked. It was obvious Flix didn't want to run through the office, but he crawled on four paws to the next corner.

What now? Was he able to put weight back on this leg?

I was hardly ever more embarrassed at the vet than at this time, which I expressed to the young veterinarian. He said that nobody ever showed up at the emergency service for no reason. We would take a very close look at him, and keep Flix's medical history in mind. When you end up in emergency, there's always a reason. Orthopedically, all tests came back OK, and the leg wasn't warm either. Was it warm before? I wasn't sure, but I didn't think so. I told the vet that I wasn't able to really touch it, and he didn't put that leg down.

The vet then took a closer look at Flix's medical history: the slightly increased kidney test levels and the intestinal inflammation from half a year ago. We had gotten that under control since then. He explained to me that this leg phenomenon could be caused by an enlarged heart; by not pumping as well it slowed down the blood stream, which could lead to a clot formation in the enlarged heart chambers. If clots then entered the bloodstream, one could get stuck somewhere; if in a leg, it could lead to paralysis and the cat wouldn't be able anymore to use the limb. But, it could at first just make limbs "fall asleep in an extreme way" and make it temporarily impossible to use them, which in Flix's case seemed to have resolved itself two hours after the event at home.

Long story short: We drove back home, happy that nothing worse had come from this event, but with the recommendation to have a heart ultrasound exam done.

We got home, told Max for the first time what had happened, and we all then cuddled on the sofa. What a day ...

It was definitely necessary that Sylvia had a talk with Flix. Here are a few excerpts of what Flix had to tell us:

Flix feels "tingly" under his skin, so nervous, like hair standing up on his back, somewhat tense, strained, not relaxed, and I believe he sits around a lot with sunken shoulders and making himself smaller than he is. As if he would retreat into his own little world to protect himself ...

Little Flix feels a little sad at the moment. Somehow "put away" and hidden in his own world. When I ask him why, he tells me it has to do with the energies (atmospheric disturbances), the tingling in the air and the noises and feelings. He doesn't feel secure right now, as it happened once before, and it is a very old fear that creeps up from inside of him. The energies, the heavy air, the unease around him that you can't see but feel as if the space around you is "burning," that is what scares him. And he feels much safer in a protected room, a retreating area with "with walls surrounding him."

He says it also affects him physically and he doesn't feel very good then, it's like he can't breathe (circulation? heart?) and this tingling inside of him, this uneasiness which affects his whole body (nervous system) and puts pressure on his head (like a headache, particularly on the left). And then he feels cold and colder and his body stiffens.

Then, when you or Max come to him and comfort him and take him out, it's all much better. Other than that, he feels pretty left alone at the moment. Yes, sometimes by Max. (He really needs someone who takes care of him and gives him the security he needs every moment, takes him out of his hiding place, provides protection and lends a hand, communicates and confirms that everything is OK, and does it again and again).

Quite suddenly, he became very worried about Max; was afraid he wouldn't come back, because everything is so uneasy at the moment out there and this fear arose in him like a strange premonition that something was about to happen ... but I also sense a little bit of jealousy deep inside of him when Max receives this special attention (when he needs to see the vet etc.) and Flix then feels left alone and passed by. When he came out of the storage closet and screamed, it was a big cry for help.

"Take care of me, I really really need you right now." Yes, his foot had fallen asleep, but it wasn't just that. It was a reason to get the full attention that he now needs so much and that Max doesn't give him to the degree he did before.

Yes, Tamara, now it's much more expected of you to get him, get him out of the closet, talk to him, comfort him, hold him, provide protection and security and love, much more of all of it at the moment! Because he needs it right now and then his world will be saner and he'll manage the energies better and I hope with the weather calming down, his physical condition and fears will calm as well.

Thank you Flix, you wonderful soul!

———————

As always, when the results of the animal communication arrive, it tugs at my heartstrings and I shed a lot of tears; because I am so moved and because of my never-ending love for my cats. I could beat myself up for apparently having neglected him, or having instilled these feelings of neglect in him. As he usually did during this time, he sat in the storage closet when we received Sylvia's information. So, I sat down next to him and we had a very long talk and we cuddled. I assured him that he is the most perfect of all black-and-white tomcats, that I love him very much and that I never wanted to neglect him. I also explained to him that Max just needed a lot of energy for himself, and I needed a lot of time caring for Max. Dental surgery at his age was no easy task. Then, I was able to convince Flix to come out with me.

Next, I spoke with Max and explained to him how Flix was apparently feeling. We all had missed the opportunity to involve him earlier, and in a better way, in the events. I asked Max to look after Flix a little more often now, and to convey to him that we are always here for him, and that at he is protected and loved every moment of the day and night.

As I had thought already: Max understood every word. In the afternoon, he was all of a sudden sitting in front of the storage closet, looking out for Flix. My Max, my wise soul. I loved them both so much.

That gave Flix the protection and security that he had missed so much last week.

I sat down next to Flix in the storage closet, and we cuddled and talked. Max joined us, with a controlling look on his face: "Whatever this is shaping up to be, should you need me, I am here for you!" He sat down on my gym bag with the typical proud presence of his, and looked at Flix and me in a probing but also very competent way.

These events tugged on my heart a lot, and they went to the core of my sensitivity. I am at least as sensitive as my little Flix. Not only in this situation did I recognize in him a mirror to myself. I am also very sensitive as far as energies are concerned. I always sense when energy levels are changing. The fact that Flix suffered a lot from these changes affected me strongly. It also made me sad and somewhat helpless.

Little Flix is such a sensitive and vulnerable soul, and I love him very much. I see so much of myself in him. I know exactly when the moments occur during which Max is stealing the show from him. Not because that was his goal, but because Max is simply Max. Just what you expect from an alpha type. Max doesn't let anything spoil his day, not even his CKD. I learn so much from him as well.

We had planned a long weekend, visiting friends in England. I wrestled with this for a long time; whether I should go on the trip or not. Flix was improving a lot; he liked his cat sitter who would come twice every day. Maybe a little bit of distance would do us all good?

Reluctantly, we went on our journey. And lo and behold, when we came back on Sunday evening, we found cats that were very relaxed. Everything was good.

After we were home again, we received flower essences sprays made from Australian bush flowers. Flower essences are safe and effective in unlocking inherent positive qualities such as love, courage, and joy. The sprays helped a lot. I used this protective spray to cover all Flix's places so he would feel protected and secure wherever he sat or lay. This contact spray enhanced trust, which was good for the both of us. It was supposed to be sprayed over his paws. But that wasn't easily accomplished. So, I first sprayed my hands and then dabbed his paws with it. He found that interesting and somehow exciting.

One little step at a time, Flix came out of his depressive phase. Little by little, he participated in our life again. Slowly his joy of living returned along with the bright glow in his eyes.

His eyes always reflected very openly, just as mine, what his soul was feeling. They again reflected the radiance of a soul that loves and is being loved, that trusts and is at peace with itself. The beautiful depth also returned to his gleaming eyes, showing the deepness of a very sensitive soul that has arrived and simply "is." And with that, his love for playing came back as well.

FLIX'S HEART

O ur next step was to determine the health of Flix's heart. Because of the temporarily paralyzed front leg and our emergency visit, I made an appointment for an ultrasound exam. Our vet at the clinic is specialized in cardiology, so she was the best person to go to.

After the experience with Max's CKD, I did my research before the visit and looked for possible causes. I learned which heart conditions had to be considered for older cats, what the symptoms are, and how the condition could be diagnosed.

HCM, hypertrophic cardiomyopathy, was the name of the scary disease. It is an increase in the size of the heart. What can happen, unfortunately not infrequently, is that the enlarged atrium causes more clots to form. If a clot forms, comes loose, and gets into the blood circulation, it warrants the highest level of alert. These clots usually become attached to a point on the main artery, the aorta, which is responsible for the blood supply to the hind legs. If such an aortic thrombosis develops, it can lead to immediate paralysis in the hind limbs and immense pain. This is usually the death sentence for the affected cat.

Mike, a dear friend in England, had lost his 15-year-old cat to that condition just a few weeks ago. Therefore, it was very important to clear up the situation.

Flix's vet explained to me that we would examine the two atria (the upper chambers) of the heart. If they were OK, meaning not enlarged, we would be able to stop the ultrasound right away.

And as luck had it, that's how it went: Flix's heart was healthy! I drove home very relieved. For Flix, this was an especially good experience because no one stuck a needle in his body.

I can't even describe what a great weight had been lifted from me. Everything was good. We had accompanied him and helped him out of his depression, and he enjoyed life again. And his heart was healthy! My joy knew no bounds!

The paralyzed leg had just been an extremely painful limb that had fallen asleep. Or, it was the harbinger of things to come a half year from now. But one thing at a time!

Intuition as Guiding Element

Now I was so impressed by the animal communication and its results that I signed up for Sylvia's introductory course.

At the same time, I was already participating in a spiritual leadership program which was held in Scotland, with four one-week modules over the course of almost two years.

Why did I sign up for this program? I followed my intuition as the program was led by two teachers, Peggy Dylan and Stephen Mulhearn, that I already worked with over the last couple of years. A huge part of my spiritual development was, at this time, inspired by them. The program's goal was to awaken the students' inner potential so that we could grow personally, and develop the capability to lead from the heart; to lead with a spiritual, holistic perspective in mind.

In addition, I had received my soul reading and soul level clearing in mid-April from Toby Alexander. The depth of information that was unearthed there—all revealed through the Akashic Records, the energetic database of each individual soul—impressed me very much and influenced my further personal growth in a decisive way. How did I meet Toby? This is really funny and shows how small our world is and that there are no coincidences. A spiritual workshop participant I met years ago, who then moved to Tanzania, sent me a link to a webinar on DNA activation in 2015. I was immediately deeply impressed by the depth of Toby's work and the holistic, scientific background of his teachings, as well as the effectiveness of his programs. I decided to work with Toby within seconds, following my intuition.

I wanted to learn everything about soul insights, energetic clearing, and DNA activation. But first, my intuition said that I had to tackle the animal communication.

Apropos intuition: All of this may sound strange to you if you are a mental-rational person who has a hard time believing in intuition in the first place. Let me quickly explain three terms—instinct, intellect, and intuition—so you can better understand what's required to have conversations with animals.

Instinct belongs to the body. Instinct is when your body functions automatically. You don't need to take care of your breathing, of your blood circulation, and millions of other processes in your body. Your instinct takes care of it.

Intuition belongs to your soul. Intuition is when your soul functions automatically. Intuition is when you receive insights and information from your Higher Self, from your soul. It's this subtle feeling, which is often called "gut feeling" (which is actually a "heart feeling"). It's your intuition that leads you to make a choice that may seem "unreasonable," but your life changes forever for the better. It's intuition to choose a spiritual teacher. Your soul knows who your teacher should be and when a new teacher arises at your horizon. It's intuition if you feel guided to do this or to stop doing that. Intuition has no problems. Intuition has solutions. Intuition is not tangible, which is exactly what drives the intellect crazy. Because the intellect wants to explain, to define, to isolate, to calculate, etc.

Intellect sits in between instinct and intuition. It's the human mind, the rational mind. If you look at our educational systems, then you can clearly see that they are very focused on building the intellect only. Science is based on intellect only. The intellect knows "facts" which leads to the phenomenon that the intellect can only give old answers to new questions.

Of course, your intellect can help you a lot. As a servant, but not as a master.

Back to the animal communication course. I really enjoyed Sylvia's first course. In fact, we were having conversations with our animals, and animals of other participants, from day one. The trick was to shut off the brain so much that intuition became the guiding element. On this basis, we connected energetically with the animals and were able to receive information from the animals. Based on this, we were to keep practicing and then begin the structured training. Oh yes, I would do exactly that!

The day was focused on a lot of practice. We did exercises and meditations that helped us to let the mind (the intellect) be a servant only, and to make our intuition the guiding principle. We started to work with sending information and receiving information telepathically. We began by sending a color to another participant and they had to "decode" the information. It was stunning how well that worked. Then, we had to send information about where we live, and we worked on that. Next, we entered into a meditation to become the animal we wanted to talk to, and built a heart-to-heart-connection to the animal; like building an energetic signal line.

In the next phase, we were divided into groups of four. Each person could practice with their own and three other animals. Sylvia supported each group, verifying our results. It was amazing. In some situations, I was blocked and didn't get anything. And in other situations, when I could better allow my intuition to kick in, it worked much better.

Animals are mainly guided by their instincts and their intuition. That's why they appreciate it so much when humans learn to use intuition to communicate. Finally, they are heard!

EAR INFECTION

In August 2016, I went to Scotland for the third module of my spiritual leadership program. Toward the end of the week, on Friday morning, I woke up with pain in my left ear. The pain lasted the whole day. Very unusual, since I hardly ever experience pain in my ears. Except in the wintertime, when they hurt on the outside, due to the overwhelming cold.

That evening when I called Michael, who had stayed at home with the cats, he told me that he had been to the veterinary clinic because Max's left ear had become infected. Yes, you guessed it: his left ear. My pain had abated when I found out about it. Souls that are connected to each other are continuously exchanging energies. I was very moved by the experiences I had. We were energetically connected to each other across space and time.

Back home again, Max's ear didn't get better but worse. There was very dark ear wax which led to more and more scabs. I got the sinking feeling that we weren't doing the right thing with the current treatment.

Since the time that Max lived with us, he had sometimes had the habit of scratching his left ear. Much more so than his right ear. I had talked about it with every vet. They all told me that "there is a lot of wax in the ear," which then was removed, but they never provided any diagnoses or conspicuous findings which would have necessitated a thorough examination. And, Max never showed any stress because of the ear. Sometimes he didn't scratch it for an entire week.

The solution used for flushing the ear was supposed to dissolve the secretion and remove it from the ear. The eardrops should bring down the swelling inside the ear. This I could of course not see for myself. But, new wax or wound secretions were forming continuously.

Kidneys and ears, ears and kidneys. Both organs are, according to Chinese medicine, connected energetically with each other. There is a correlation somehow which, at the moment, I did not yet understand. Infections of the ear can also have something to do with "not wanting to listen" or with "not being listened to." When do I not listen, or when does Max feel he's not listened to? From whatever angle I tried to understand the problem, I wasn't able to get anywhere.

His ear continued to get infected, and sometimes started bleeding. Something was waiting to be discovered here, I was quite certain about it. A case for Sylvia, a case for a shamanic healing journey.

The following Monday night, Max hid in the storage closet, which he hardly ever did. The storage closet was primarily Flix's refuge and retreat. Max was most likely mad at me because I had put a cat cone on him. I wanted to prevent him from scratching his reasonably healed ear and keep the ear from bleeding again. This was early in the week, and our appointment at the veterinary clinic was scheduled for the upcoming Friday.

The next morning, Max came to me into the bedroom and gave me a meaningful look. Without his cat cone! He did it again and had gotten rid of the collar. Then I looked a little closer: The ear was all bloody, much worse than before.

There was no time to lose. I called the clinic and described the situation. An emergency appointment the same day or an appointment with an ENT specialist the next day were our choices. Since I wanted to clean the ear at first, I decided to take the ENT appointment on Wednesday.

Then Sylvia wrote to me and told me that she had undertaken the shamanic journey with Max last night. At the end of the process a plug shot out of his ear like a cork from a champagne bottle. Aha! That's where the bloody ear came from! There was a deeper meaning for this as well.

On Wednesday in the clinic it became quite apparent that Max needed a CT scan because the vets couldn't see where the blood was coming from—the outside or the inside. Everything else, allergies and intolerances could be ruled out. The vets suspected more and more that there was a polyp or tumor in Max's ear which caused the infection, the pain and the swelling.

It turned out that the bleeding ear that occurred after the shamanic healing journey was a blessing in this situation. It paved the way for an accurate diagnosis. The vets shifted their focus from a simple, perhaps protracted, ear infection to something bigger that they needed to pin down.

Since Max needed to be put under for the CT scan, and anesthesia for cats with chronic kidney disease needed some preparation, I wanted to wait for the regular kidney check-up on the following Friday. It would provide a complete blood panel and kidney diagnosis update. At that visit, the blood levels were quite stable, "badly stable" from a kidney perspective, as my vet commented. However, she also advised to schedule the CT scan and then have the surgery right after that; so Max, in case surgery was necessary, would only need one anesthesia. She said that any ear condition could become worse than doing the anesthesia and operation now. The big day would be early next week. We shouldn't do anything to the ear until then.

So we went home, Max and me. As always, we discussed the situation on our way home. Max complained loudly about the whole day; he really didn't like it at all. It was all too annoying, too stressful and completely unnecessary anyway.

Max was supposed to enjoy the next few days at home as much as possible, to be in the best possible shape on the day of the surgery. September was very sunny, Max spent a lot of time on the balcony, lying in the sun and pondering. At the same time, he dutifully took all his kidney medication, his medicinal mushrooms, his globules and his homeopathic complex remedy.

The day was drawing near. On the day, Max could not eat or drink until I took him to the clinic at 12:30 p.m. He would be given infusions for the next three hours to prepare the kidneys as best as possible for the anesthesia. I had already been told that he would have to stay one night at the clinic should the surgery be necessary, because of infusions and pain therapy.

We still had a few minutes to ourselves in the consulting room. I took him out of his cat carrier and onto my lap. I told myself just transfer a lot of love to him, so he'll be OK after everything he might have to go through. At that moment, it was already clear to both of us that he wouldn't just need a CT scan.

Intuitively, I sang for him, a "native American song" which I had learned at the seminar in Scotland. This was the energy that my soul received at this particular moment. Max relaxed and snuggled up to me and we held each other and absorbed the wonderful energy of this song. This was one of the most tender moments that both of us had ever experienced.

Then came the moment when I had to hand him over to the vets. Together with my old sleeping shirt which now belonged to him, and his first toy that he had gotten from us: a pillow filled with spelt, with a snuggle face on it. Take care, my wonderful Max; I'm going to pick you up again tomorrow and I'm always with you anyway! And then we'll drive home together again. Everything will be OK.

A Tumor in the Ear

At home I tried to go about my work, which was pretty hard to do. The CT examination was scheduled for 4 p.m. At the same time, I went into a healing "Om Mane Padme Hum Meditation" for him. The "Om Mane Padme Hum" mantra is the mantra of compassion and healing. I accompanied it with music and used it for my meditation for Max. It creates a wonderful energy that I wanted to convey to Max. And to my nerves too.

Then came the time to wait. A call. The veterinary clinic. A tumor in the ear. They didn't know yet if it was benign or malignant, only that it had to be extracted. Somehow I already knew that. Still, you hope until the end that it will be something very simple. Here, too, I was in a kind of "autopilot mode." I had feared it. So, the ear infection wasn't just an ear infection. It drew our attention to the real problem, the ear tumor. I had asked the vet what she would do if it were her cat. She said she would operate immediately because there was no alternative. OK. Then please get started right away. So, Max had to go through another surgery. The second surgery in a year. My beloved Max. Hopefully things would again improve after that.

Meanwhile, I had read up on ear tumors in cats. The bad news is they are often malignant. The good news they seldom metastasize. The vet who performed the surgery pointed out to me that she had noticed a left lymph node on the left side of his neck was swollen. I should keep an eye on it.

Then I had to wait again. One hour went by. No call. Even after two hours, no call. Why had I forgotten to ask how long the procedure would take? My own fault, I knew it.

Shortly before 8 p.m., the call came in from the clinic. Max was awake and was playing with the infusion tubes. A good sign when he keeps the staff busy. The surgery went great, they were able to extract the tumor and it was sent to the pathology lab for further examination. They would call again tomorrow to let me know when I could pick him up.

Flix and I cuddled and played a lot that night. We missed Max. Very much. The way he would busily patrol his territory; just his being here which always made us experience joy, happiness and appreciation. Flix was missing his compass, his buddy, his protector and adviser. And I missed Max, my beloved Max, the best in the world.

GOING HOME AND ONTO
THE BALCONY

I was told to pick Max up the next day. I received the call in the late morning, after the check-up and the final exams had gone well.

In the early afternoon, I went to the clinic to pick up my brave fighter. I was full of joy and positive feelings. The vet explained everything that I should pay attention to, which medication he would need for the next few days, and how I should administer it.

She also explained to me that he had what is known as Horner's Syndrome on his left eye. This occurs when nerves in the eye area are also injured during the surgery on the ear, which cannot be avoided when removing a tumor from the ear canal. I should be prepared that his left eye would look different now. No problem, I had read about it already and learned that only time could help, and the eye could get back to normal again.

With all things packed up, I went to pay and then waited for Max. I sat there for a few minutes. No Max. Five minutes passed. Then ten minutes. Max still hadn't been brought in. I felt a slight panic. Something was wrong here ... I asked them where Max was now. Good question, said the receptionist, she'll have a look, she said. He will be brought out in a moment. OK. Several more minutes passed. No Max in sight. Then finally, the door opened and they brought him. He had just peed himself on his sleeping shirt, actually my sleeping shirt, and his toy had yet to be found. Pure relief! Yes, if that was the only little problem ...

So Max and I went home. As always, we discussed the situation on the way home. But this time Max was very quiet. He had to wear a cat cone again and looked at me with big eyes. "Why this again?" he seemed to be saying. "OK, the aching ball of yarn is gone from my ear now, but wearing something like this again? Really ... how could you let that happen? I really don't like it ... besides, something is wrong with my eye ..."

I understood this only all too well. My poor Max. The things he already had gone through. This had been the third time under full anesthesia within twelve months, and the second one this year. Now it was important to focus our energies on Max's recovery.

The final September days were warm and sunny; terrific for recovering from the strains of surgery. When we got home, he wanted to immediately go out on the balcony into the sunshine. Relieved, he went outside, and for starters, he just sat down and looked around his territory. He seemed reassured that certain things hadn't changed.

I used the next couple of days to establish a routine again. As soon as there was sunshine on the balcony in the late morning, I got his lawn chair ready and he could go outside, lie down comfortably on his chair, and enjoy the warm sunlight shining on his silky red fur. He sat there for hours, like a king holding court, and meditating.

THE TUMOR WAS MALIGNANT

A little more than a week later, the veterinary clinic called to inform me about the pathological findings. The tumor in Max's ear had been malignant, as are about 90% of all cat tumors. Still, we were lucky because the doctor had been able to remove the tumor in its entirety. And, these types of tumors would only in rare cases metastasize.

From the ear infection to the CT scan, from the suspicion of the tumor to the operation with subsequent diagnosis of malignancy, there wasn't much time to think about it. Rather, quick decisions were required, combined with the hope that this would solve the problem. Only now have I been able to really think about cancer. What would be the long-term effects of removing the tumor? Unfortunately, along with the tumor, the ear canal also had to be removed. So Max wouldn't be able to hear anything in that left ear. How fortunate that he was with us. In the wild, such limited ability would quickly be life-threatening.

For the next few weeks, everything revolved around Max's recovery. My focus was on letting him regain his strength quickly and getting his Horner Syndrome under control. Again, it became obvious how incredibly brave Max was, how much he was able to endure and overcome, and how well he adjusted to the situation. He now had no fur around his left ear and on that side of his neck. It looked like he had a Mohawk. Then there was the Horner Syndrome of the left eye. In the beginning, it looked like

... well, we had to get used to it. The eye looked smaller because it seemed to be farther back in the eye socket. And the pupil looked different, slightly turned. Not easy to deal with.

Of course, I wanted to treat him as normally as possible. I had to try hard not to focus my attention solely on the eye with the Horner Syndrome.

This time, we had to be careful to keep the cat cone on for at least a week. The sutures were much bigger than those for both dental surgeries. And, we really didn't want them ripped out. He received pain medication, again an opioid due to his CKD, an antibiotic, and his regular medicine for the kidneys. This kept us busy around the clock.

After this most recent surgery, Max clearly needed more time to recover. The procedure had been much more difficult than the dental restorations. He showed himself to be a real fighter again, competent, and having everything under control. As always, he wanted to be our rock that we could lean on. He just couldn't resume his old eating habits. He ate less than before the surgery, no matter what we served him. At that point, he received several different types of food, and he was supposed to eat what he liked. He was fed kidney food (mainly because he liked it so much) and high-quality food with moderate protein content, which we used with phosphate binders, so his kidneys could handle it.

After ten days, Michael took him to the follow-up appointment since I had to travel to England on business. Those two did an excellent job; his cat cone was newly adjusted and his kidney function levels were checked. And, no one had expected this: the creatinine levels had come down significantly after the surgery. They hadn't been that low in a whole year! Wow. None of the vets could explain how this was possible and whether or not it was connected to the tumor in the ear. But it didn't matter. Most important was that at this point, we could heave a sigh of relief. In any case, the combination of healing mushrooms and his homeopathic complex medication seemed to help a lot. And, the removal of the core of the infection—yes, a tumor always has to do with infection—could only have positive effects for the kidneys.

Pajama Parts and Paper Balls

We don't know much about Max's past except for what he revealed via animal communication in the chapter "King of the Strays." We can assume that his long life on a farm kept him from getting neutered for a long time.

Max had taken a special liking to the top part of one of my old pajama sets. I had not meant to throw it out yet. But, I let him have it when he requested it. He enjoyed tremendously carrying this piece around with him, finding a corner and having fun with it as cats would. That meant he still had a lot of testosterone in his body.

Every few days he looked for this top and walked around the apartment with it. I kept putting it upstairs in the bedroom so he could find it easily. He took it in his mouth and usually went down the stairs with it. He did all that very skillfully, never tripping over his paws.

Every now and then, he would walk to his food with the pajama top in his mouth, put it down and take a bite to eat. Then he took it back in his mouth and went to a corner and played with it.

Max had developed this habit early on and kept it almost to the end, even in the last weeks of his life. It gave me a clear signal that Max was living in the here and now, and that he was enjoying life in the best way possible in the moment.

Another one of his likes was to be the best goalie in the paper ball game. I don't remember exactly how it all came about. At some point, I took filling paper from a package, crumpled it up and playfully tossed it to him. I wanted to see if he liked it.

Max wasn't one to touch traditional cat toys. Well, I think he wasn't familiar with them. And, he found it undignified to chase a fishing rod or a string. Flix, on the other hand, liked it very much. Flix also liked his snuggle toys and cat nip. But for Max, it was a strange world. He preferred more practical things. Like pajama tops and paper balls.

So we started to play with paper balls. We practiced "shooting at the goal wall." For that, Max took up his position on the little red carpet we had in the hallway. He was the goalie so-to-speak. We threw paper balls at him and he became really good at catching them. He enjoyed it immensely. And so did we. Particularly, his Cat Dad had quite a few wonderful moments playing the paper ball game. Michael now started to call Max "Max Neuer," referring to Germany's national soccer goalkeeper Manual Neuer.

THE LYMPH NODE
ISN'T LOOKING GOOD

Signs that Max's recovery would take longer were already visible and palpable. He ate less for weeks and didn't resume his usual portion size. And, he lost weight as a result. From his 13 lbs. he came down to 12 lbs. Once again it became clear how good it was that he had some fat reserves, despite all the admonitions I had to listen to about Max's weight when the two cats came to us. In his prime, he was just a very handsome tomcat. For good reasons, as we could now clearly see.

Over and over, I remembered the vet's words when she had operated on him: "Has anyone ever looked at the lymph node? It's swollen!" Since he was shaved around the left ear and the left side of the neck anyway, it was easy to find and feel it. I didn't like what I felt. The thing was there. Noticeable. Not big, but it couldn't be overlooked. A little too big in my book. You could literally twist and turn it as you wanted; Max's lymph node was even more swollen after the surgery. No one could say what it was like before. Nobody had noticed it before, us included.

By early November, I had my first advanced seminar on animal communication. Because of what was happening with Max, I had brought pictures of him to get information about his current state of health. What I, the other participants, and also Sylvia learned from Max was very clear: He feels different things in his left ear. Sometimes he feels a pull, sometimes it rings, sometimes he feels pressure or has a numb feeling. There was also pressure behind the left eye. He made it clear that he needed vitamin B for the myelin sheaths of the nerve endings. Sylvia, who got this information from him, said herself: "Let's Google that and see what he means exactly." This statement from him that he needed vitamin B shows the immense knowledge that animals have. We humans can only benefit if we listen to them more often and with more attention. Interestingly, no one heard him complain about pain from his lymph node.

The whole area in and around the operated ear and the eye continued to be problematic, and he was still struggling with Horner's syndrome. Otherwise he was happy; he said that he needed time, but that otherwise he enjoyed the close relationship with us and just lived in the moment. "Love is so beautiful," he stated as well. My beloved Max!

On our way back home from the seminar I decided to make an appointment with the veterinary clinic to clarify his feeling in the area of his ear, and to have the lymph node examined.

It was now mid-November and he was given an appointment right away. The swollen lymph node was not benign. The biopsy had revealed that it wasn't a new cancer but a metastasis of the malignant ear tumor. So much for the facts, for the pathology.

The emotional perception is completely different than just hearing the facts. The vet, the young ENT surgeon who had done Max's operation, could hardly believe it herself. When she came back from the biopsy exam to the consulting room and gave me the bad news, she was so sad and upset that I burst into tears without warning. I cry easily anyway, and it doesn't take much at all to get my tears flowing.

"What would you recommend?" I asked her, in tears. Well, we could try chemo, but then there's his CKD, so no. Radiation could be done, but no, his CKD ... Ultimately, the sick kidneys could immediately thwart our plans for any form of therapy.

Even if his kidneys had rebounded after the tumor had been extracted from his body, Max's CKD was of course not gone. The blood test numbers were better, but still significantly high. He was and remained in IRIS Stage III[1] out of four stages. So, we had to be careful regarding his kidneys.

---

1. The International Renal Interest Society (IRIS) differentiates between four stages of CRF with defined diagnoses and therapeutic proposals. More on this in the appendix.

Without another thought, it was immediately clear to me that I would not expose him to radiation, not under any circumstances. And certainly no further surgery. Especially since no one had reliable data about his chances of recovery. My brave fighter, my Max, had already undergone three surgeries in twelve months. And the last one was no small feat ...

What other alternatives were there? Cortisone therapy, Metacam therapy—a pain reliever that can also slow down tumor growth. No, none of it is good with this CKD. The vet wanted to consult her supervisor as well, and once more go over all the options with him. We agreed to speak on the phone the next day.

Max immediately sensed that something wasn't good at all. He wanted to see me laughing, in a good mood, with inner joy. I know that. At that moment, there was only deep sadness and a certain powerlessness, and this pain that I would probably lose Max soon. Max curled up in his carrier. I took him out, took him in my arms, and just held him. Just held him. Breath in, breath out. Breath in, breath out. Until we were in the same rhythm of breathing. All of this just couldn't be true ...

I encouraged both of us that everything would be fine. And, that we both would show everyone, especially the cancer, that we were fighters.

The vet assured me that I could sit there with Max as long as I wanted. She asked me to leave when I was ready, not earlier.

So, we sat alone in the consulting room for a while. It was a special combination of feelings, a very deep love, much togetherness, intimacy, and of course a lot of sadness. And then there was the feeling of powerlessness. Finally, I put Max back in his carrier and we left. I went home in tears and somewhat in a trance. I even forgot to pay the bill. Of course, we did that afterwards.

Whenever Max and I drove home from the vet, he usually "texted" me. In the car he usually said to me what he wanted to say the whole time: that he thought this day, especially the vet visit, was a pretty stupid idea. Especially after the dental surgeries, when he was given an opioid pain reliever, he was usually very talkative.

Today he was quiet, completely withdrawn, and it was very hard for me to hide my tears. I just couldn't do it. I was infinitely sad ... and so my tears flowed. I explained to Max that my tears had primarily to do with me and the whole unfortunate situation. Just like the way he hisses to himself at the vet to deal with his stress, tears flow from me. I'm not that good at hissing ...

During our ride home, I discussed with him what we should do to best help him. I also told him that I just can't help but let my tears run free; that I love him, love him very much, and would do anything to help him as best as possible. That I'll fight alongside of him if he wants to fight. That I will do my research to find the best possible solution for his situation, for him.

When we got home, Max first had to recover from today's trip to the veterinary clinic. It was our last trip to the veterinary clinic together. Without the very competent and committed team at the Hofheim Veterinary Clinic, we would never have gotten Max's CKD so well under control.

I kept thinking about the first vet, who had treated him completely wrong. In spring 2015 he said "I can't do more for him." If we had stayed with this vet, Max would have probably been dead already for a while.

Luckily, we came to the Hofheim Veterinary Clinic. In this case, the statistics should have been on our side, since 90% of such tumors do *not* metastasize. Well, for us, it was different. Pointless to ponder, because it was quite clear again that general numbers are of no use at all in a specific individual case.

It was more important to very quickly find a good way to help Max.

WHICH THERAPY IS RIGHT FOR MAX?

Max's first reaction at home was to withdraw. I'm sure he had a talk with Flix. I immediately started looking for alternative cancer therapies for cats. Mycotherapy, with which we had already experienced good results with the kidneys, was the first remedy that came to mind.

As is so often the case, the right people come into one's life when the time is right. When I searched the internet, I actually found a veterinarian near us who, in addition to other alternative healing methods and conventional medicine, had also been offering mycotherapy for a short time. I called right away and was able to talk to at once with the vet herself. Yes, she said, there are chances; I should send her the findings and the pathology report in advance. But she immediately pointed out to me that mycotherapy alone would not suffice. We made an appointment for Tuesday.

Of course, I consulted the group for cats with kidney disease, asked who had the combination of CKD and cancer to see how others dealt with it and what options there were.

A valued comrade-in-arms who lost one of her tomcats to a nasal tumor recommended an animal health practitioner who worked holistically from a distance. I contacted him as well. After an in-depth exchange, he created a therapy plan for me, which also changed the previous CKD therapy. This plan was fundamentally different. It was a good plan; just a big change for which I would have preferred the therapist close by.

After the appointment with the new vet the following week, it was clear that Max and I would work with her. She was as calm as it seemed possible. She recommended a combination of organotherapy, a kind of live-cell therapy that reminds the cells of what their real task is; and mycotherapy since, as she said, we needed to get the tumor under control quickly in order to have a real chance. Max felt comfortable with her. Well, he wasn't thrilled, but I knew his expression when visiting a vet.

She advised against changing all existing therapeutic approaches in his condition, especially not all at once. In this complex situation, she explained that too much change could bring the system from neutral status to a crash. Of course, that was to be avoided. So, the new medicinal mushrooms against cancer were used with great caution. He was given his organotherapy injection twice a week initially, later once a week. This therapy would always be adapted to his current state of health.

You might be wondering why I wouldn't have tried other approaches, like snake venom or apricot kernel extracts. A brief overview: Special apricot kernel extracts contain amygdalin—not to be confused with potassium cyanide and free hydrogen cyanide—which has the potential to destroy cancer cells. This is a phytotherapeutical approach. Snake venom is known to some of you as Horvi Enzyme Therapy. The aim here is to obtain pure toxins from raw toxins taken from snakes, spiders, or scorpions. Each pure toxin contains many enzymes that are active against cancer cells, among other things. I've read nearly everything. I even bought apricot kernels from a colleague and brought them home as a precaution. But, I do not have snake poisons at home—no worries.

So, there were many options. I just had to make a quick *and* workable decision. Every day of delay, every day of indecision on my part, could be one day too many. Given Max's overall condition, three surgeries in twelve months, the CKD, and the still existing Horner syndrome in the eye, it was important to have a veterinarian by my side who offered a lot of alternative methods. I never before had cared for a cancer patient, human or animal.

Therefore, I wanted to have someone close by whom I could trust and with whom I could work closely. This vet was only ten minutes away. I preferred that to a therapist who was three hours away; that just didn't seem practical in our situation. At that time, I couldn't imagine Max's therapy being managed "remotely."

What was workable and in which option did I have the most confidence? What was best for Max's ailing overall system? That was the bottom line, because every situation is slightly different, just like every cat is slightly different. The path you take has to be one that you trust and believe in. Your path with your cat may look very different than mine, and that's perfectly fine. Because your situation is different. On principle, and not only in this case, I have stopped thinking in categories like "right" and "wrong." In Max's case, the oncologists at the veterinary clinic and this new vet agreed that conventional medicine should not be followed because of his CKD.

In such situations you have to make quick decisions. I made a fundamental decision that it should be a therapy that supported his immune system and him as a whole being, while also targeting cancer cells. So, the combination of organotherapy and medicinal mushrooms made sense to me.

HOW DOES ONE HANDLE THIS

The diagnosis of the metastasis overwhelmed me completely. Boom. Right in the heart. Nothing was as before. Knocked me out. The diagnosis hit exactly at the point when it seemed we had solved the situation with the ear surgery. But no, we hadn't. We had just been given another mountain to climb.

On Wednesday, we went to the veterinary clinic for the diagnosis, and on Thursday I had to go on a workshop tour for two days; first to Nuremberg, then from there directly to Stuttgart. There was no getting around it. The dates were confirmed and we had to keep them. I've always been very disciplined, and it was the same here. Care for our cats was arranged, Michael would work from home. But, it was unbelievably difficult for me to go and leave my Max behind.

I got in the car on Thursday morning to be in Nuremberg for the first workshop in the afternoon. It took about three hours to get there, so I had a lot of time to think. And that was good. I couldn't help myself and first let my tears flow freely. I was sure I would be able to make myself presentable again by the afternoon.

When I get into situations like this, I first have to cry all the tears my heart forces me to cry. Without doing it, I can't go on to the next phase. That of reflecting, of thinking about what exactly triggered me in such a way, in order to then enter the phase of decision-making. And that was the most important thing: making the right decisions. Just like with the CKD, when Max's situation was dire, I suddenly realized that his life depended on my decisions. And directly so.

Whatever I couldn't cry out yesterday had to be "cried away" now. I was infinitely sad because I suddenly realized that my time with Max, this wonderful cat, was finite. Very finite. Very limited. Was it a matter of months or just weeks? Then again, the question was: what had changed since yesterday? Nothing except that I had gained knowledge of something that had already been there before. Only before, it was called "swollen lymph nodes." Since the diagnosis it was called "metastasis." That was the whole difference. It was a metastasis from the start. Even before anyone could have seen it with their eyes.

I thought for a long time that it was a wonderful example of quantum physics, which says that we influence our reality through our observation. The facts were all exactly the same yesterday. I only knew about them since the appointment with the vet. That made all the difference. That started everything, the *knowledge* of the *significance* of the swollen lymph node. But the lymph node was there before. It just didn't have that name before, this "label" of metastasis, cancer.

And knowing about the metastasis was linked to very clear patterns that are permanently impressed upon our society: Cancer is bad, it is a matter of life and death, and if you have metastasis, then mostly you have lost the battle. What does that do to you? It's scary. Fear is rampant and seems to control you. Is it at all possible to make decisions controlled by such fear? I don't think it is. If you feel a lot of fear, then mentally you are in the future that doesn't exist yet. Not in the here and now. Fear prevents you from trusting in the here and now, and making decisions on that basis.

This reaction occurs despite the fact that, in principle, cancer can be healed. Our body fights malignant cells every day, and in most cases has no problem controlling them; that means destroying them. We don't ever notice it.

But—and this is important for the perception and handling of the diagnosis of cancer—the CKD Max had was and still is a fatal disease. It's just that when CKD is diagnosed, we're not going through the same emotional patterns that occur when the diagnosis is cancer. And, that's something we humans do. These are thought patterns that are widespread and accepted in society. With cancer, all alarms go off. Fear and panic spread. Fear can lead to shock, paralysis, and inability to act.

When we went to our first vet, I never had this thought of finiteness, the fear of loss, even though Max was facing CKD. I put him back in the carrier, went home with him and thought to myself "They'll never see us again." I took up the challenge, took full responsibility, tapped into my network, and had a lot of conversations during the next few days. Max only wanted one thing: he wanted to live! To finally be happy in his new home! Within four weeks, we had clarity, a new therapy, and things were progressing in a positive way—although we already knew then that CKD was a fatal disease. But now, the perception was a completely different one.

Those days in November 2016 were very intense. The two days that I was gone and had to hold workshops were, all in all, pretty good. I was able to go through my sadness, my powerlessness, and my fear of losing Max far away from home. I also knew that I had to be emotionally at peace with myself before returning home. Only that way could I provide the best possible support to Max. It was my job and responsibility to give him the best possible support on his path. No matter if it was going to be difficult for me. That wasn't important now. I just had to cope with it all, learn from it and grow personally from it. It was about his life. To make his life as comfortable as possible. For that I would do everything in my power. He had only been with us for less than two years.

The vet who did Max's surgery had called back; she had discussed the findings with her supervisor, one of the country's oncological experts. He also advised against conventional cancer therapy because of the CKD, Max's previous surgeries, and his current condition. Palliative therapy was one favored option. Let's do it. Well, we weren't there yet.

THE CLOCK IS TICKING

I was emotionally in a better place when I got home on Friday evening. We would now take up the fight; if and as long as Max wanted it that way! Cuddling, preparing medication and food, playing and snuggling ... that's how we started the weekend.

On Tuesday, Max and I visited the new vet. A good ten minutes through the city and we were already there. Max was allowed to stay in his carrier for now. She had read through the findings beforehand and already had a suggestion. We would inconspicuously introduce a combination of four different medicinal mushrooms, tailored to his type of cancer. But, she said that mycotherapy alone would not be enough. She recommended adding, in parallel, an organotherapy, a kind of fresh cell therapy. We would also introduce it in a staggered way.

She made it very clear that we had to get this tumor under control quickly in order to give Max a fighting chance. She also said the primary treatment goal must first be to stop the tumor from growing. Anything else, like killing the tumor, would be a bonus. Alright then, let's roll up our sleeves!

I lifted Max out of his carrier. He didn't protest at all during the exam. He didn't hiss once, which he had done off and on at the other vet.

The new vet tried to get a complete picture of the tumor. Location, size, and whether it had developed inward. Fortunately, we weren't yet facing the problem that it was growing inward. We started the organotherapy right away; Max received two subcutaneous injections. No problem. And I received the first medicinal mushroom mixture to take home with me. Over the next few days, I needed to give him an eighth of a capsule mixed in food and, after a few days, increase it to a quarter. Only then would we be sneaking in the other medicinal mushrooms as well. I built medicinal mushrooms into our routine in the morning. Max always sensed when something was good for him. So, he also took his medicinal mushrooms with a liquid recovery food that was high in calories. Super. That problem was already solved!

At the same time, Max received an energetic treatment from Sylvia. For this, I had to cut off some of the hair on his neck and send it to her with two pictures. By using these, she connected energetically with Max via pictures and neck hair, cleansed the energy field, and dissolved blockages. Every blockage prevents the animal from having available enough vital life energy. He accepted all of this very gratefully. As we would quickly find out, these therapies gave us two more months.

MAX PREPARES FOR HIS LEAVE

The next weeks weren't easy. Not for any one of us. Max felt my—our—pain, and he didn't want that. He often hid in the closet. At first, I assumed he wanted some peace and quiet. But no: as he told us via animal communication, he didn't want to see me sad. That made him sad and that's why he hid in the closet. He wanted to live in the moment, in the here and now, and fully experience every moment. He also wanted to see me and us happy. How quickly I could have misinterpreted such behavior. Because as humans, we see it from our point of view instead of the other person's or, in this case, Max's point of view. Once again I was very, very grateful for the gift of animal communication.

I tried really hard to be happy, but it was difficult for me. This situation pushed me to my limits, and beyond. Which, in the end, was a good thing. Because I grew personally a lot during these weeks. But, how much I was yet to grow, that I didn't even dare guess at this point.

Nevertheless, I also had to think of myself, of my strength. So, I treated myself to an energetic training course. I knew that I would need all my strength for Max, so I invested in myself, in a "major energetic clearing." My teacher Toby offered such a program in order to be able to start 2017 off as clear as possible without any energetic blockages. Exactly what I needed. I really enjoyed it, everything via webinar, so I could be with Max the whole time. I felt how several oppressive things fell away from me. This process also helped me greatly to perceive and accept things as they are. The fear was gone. Max would leave, but we would always stay connected. My focus was entirely on enabling him to follow his path, the path he wanted to take.

From one day to the next, Max decided that he no longer wanted to take medicinal mushrooms. He looked at what I had prepared for him, as I did for every meal: "Medicinal mushroom powder in recovery food" you could call it, or sometimes "medicinal mushroom powder in organic food." Up until now, he had happily licked it up and eaten it. But now, he looked at it and walked away, very consistently. "No, I won't take it anymore, I don't need it anymore." We had added the medicinal mushrooms, four in number, sneaked in gradually, always starting with an eighth of a capsule. But no sooner had we successfully integrated the fourth medicinal mushroom than Max decided he had enough.

One morning after Christmas, he refused to take any of it. In no way could he be convinced over the following days either. And it didn't matter which mushrooms we offered him. He had decided: No more medicinal mushrooms. I accepted it. It was his will. It was his path.

Together with our vet, we agreed that we had probably lost the fight. It was likely he would slowly start to feel pain, too. The tumor became firmer in consistency, but not really smaller. We therefore followed her recommendation to support Max from now on through palliative care. Even if the drugs we gave him weren't exactly kidney-friendly, that didn't count anymore. What was important now was his quality of life. She stated quite clearly: "He's not dying from CKD here, but from cancer."

The cancer progressed faster than the CKD. We kept the accompanying organotherapy with one injection per week. At least we wanted to try everything to support him as much as possible, because he was now losing weight and strength.

Even during this phase, Max showed astonishing clarity about the consequences of his decisions. There was no doubt and no hesitation. He made a decision, and he stuck to it.

THE YEAR 2017 STARTS VERY LIVELY

New Year's Eve is one of the worst days of the year for most animals. Few are not bothered by the explosions of firecrackers and the hissing of rockets. We experienced both cats' reactions: Max was again quite unimpressed by the noise this year while Flix, like last year, endured terrible fears. He ran from one hiding place to another. It wasn't until long after midnight that calm returned and Flix was able to relax reasonably well.

We spent the first of January helping Flix heal his fearful cat soul and preparing ourselves for the new year. Everyday life started again on January 2. In the late morning, we had an appointment for Max at the vet, where he received another organotherapy injection. When I got back with him, Flix had disappeared. He had done that several times. So, I wasn't worried at first. He often hid minutes before Max and I drove off, just to be sure that he didn't have to go with me. And he usually came out again when we were back home, and there were "no more threats" to him.

Not this time. Usually, he would join me on the sofa for a cappuccino after lunch. There was no sign of him. Neither shouts nor the clatter of cups could lure him out of his hiding place.

When he wasn't back in the early afternoon either, I became very worried. So I started turning the apartment upside down. I searched every corner, every possible hiding place; my study with all possible hideouts and Michael's office, which provided even more places to hide.

We decided to look in the storage closet, which in our apartment is a very low and sloping attic space to the right of the stairs leading to the upper floor. As you already know, this became Flix's retreat when he was in his depressive phase. Was he still so afraid of New Year's Eve? Was there something very loud after Max and I had left?

First, I removed our gym bags and a couple of cardboard boxes to get a good view of the closet and to get to the back. But no, Flix was nowhere to be seen. Not even between boxes and crates. I put everything back where it was. I desperately searched cabinets and wardrobes again. "Flix, that's not funny anymore, where are you?"

OK, he *had* to be in the storage closet. So, I started to clear out everything again. When I had uncovered a whole row of cardboard boxes, I found him: he was sitting between two cardboard boxes on the floor, frightened, as if paralyzed. Why wasn't he there before? Or had he been so far back in the corner that I didn't see him? Or did he only get into this position afterwards? Anyway ...

I picked him up, which he allowed me to do, quite surprisingly. As soon as he was outside, he wanted to run away again. Which he did.

As soon as he started running, I noticed something: Flix wasn't running smoothly, something was wrong. He was lame somehow, looked unsteady on his little legs. Sure, he must have torn a muscle when he apparently fled into the storage room in a panic. That's what I was thinking. I was going to watch him more closely.

After all the excitement of the day, it was time to relax on the sofa in the evening. Again I was amazed that I could pick Flix up without any problem, and that he stayed on my lap for a very long time by his standards. I thought it was nice at first. But, he didn't jump up anywhere that day, and then I remembered something. He hadn't jumped on his cat tree in the past few days. Right. Maybe it had nothing to do with New Year's Eve. Perhaps something else was going on here that was only masked by his fear of New Year's Eve?

The next morning, I noticed the lameness more clearly. Going to the vet with Flix is much more difficult than with Max. So, first I made a few videos to record Flix's gait pattern and sent them to the vet I trusted, who knows Flix and his fears. She called me back very late that evening and advised me to have an orthopedic surgeon and a neurologist look into it. She, herself an internist and cardiologist, had already spoken to her colleagues and she had set up an appointment with one of them. As always, her commitment was impressive. The appointment was Thursday morning at eight.

In the meantime, I had continued to deal with Flix's symptoms myself, mainly because his right hind leg was now increasingly slipping when he turned corners. I was already certain that Flix seemed to have lost his sense of balance rather than having an orthopedic problem. It was just too obvious: he wasn't running anymore either, but tried not to show any difficulty by walking very carefully. And that's not Flix. He was always the one who wandered around a lot and often raced joyfully through the whole place like a tornado. It was actually Max who walked around carefully.

Now it was time to prepare in the evening before the appointment, so that Flix could be put in the cat carrier the next morning without any problem. We had to block all "hide behind the sofa" options and close the door to the storage closet.

CLARITY ON JANUARY 5th

Without having encountered any traffic jams and stress, Flix and I arrived at the veterinary clinic at eight o'clock in the morning. The vet had already watched the videos, which turned out to be very helpful, because Flix obviously didn't feel like walking around in the consulting room. It was quickly clear that the condition was, as suspected, the so-called vestibular syndrome[1], which means loss of the sense of balance. The question was, where did this come from and how can it be treated?

There are basically several types of vestibular syndrome. Sometimes no cause can be located and the animals recover with infusions, vitamin B, and blood circulation-enhancing agents. However, there are also forms that have a clear cause that can usually be tackled. In Flix's case, the vet was able to pinpoint the cause to the head area because of his slightly odd eye movements that she had noticed, which I hadn't recognized.

---

1. vcahospitals.com: Vestibular disease is a condition in which a cat suddenly develops incoordination, falling or circling to one side, involuntary darting of the eyes back and forth (called nystagmus), a head tilt, and often nausea or vomiting. These clinical signs usually appear suddenly, often in less than an hour. Vestibular disease is a disease that can affect cats of all ages. The vestibular apparatus is located in the inner ear and is responsible for maintaining our balance, and sense of orientation and direction. Whenever the vestibular apparatus is diseased or damaged, balance and coordination are adversely affected, resulting in symptoms involving equilibrium (balance).

She recommended an MRI, in case I wanted to address the cause. Of course I wanted that. I am not a fan of treating symptoms, neither for myself nor for my animals. Until a few days ago, Flix was a lively older tomcat, estimated to be 17 years old. So, he was given a light anesthetic for the MRI, and I couldn't do anything but wait.

The MRI examination showed that he had a type of swelling or polyp in his left middle ear—yes, not only in Max's but also in Flix's left ear—which became so large that it impaired his sense of balance. When the growth became very large, Flix could no longer keep his balance. That probably happened exactly when Max and I weren't at home on Monday. There were warnings a few days before that, when Flix had already stopped jumping onto the cat tree.

The only way to cure this is through surgery, during which the tumor is removed from the ear. Anything else, such as cortisone, would only reduce symptoms. Since he had this mass in the middle ear, even infusions with vitamin B would not be very promising as a symptom treatment.

The vet also told me all other options: one was to put him to sleep. She was also clear in her message that one shouldn't leave him like that. He would suffer from permanent dizziness and would not be able to control his balance as long as the growth was in his ear.

No, euthanasia wasn't an option for me. I would never have thought of this at all. Flix was a senior cat, whether he was an estimated 17 years old or a little younger made no difference to me. Until a few days ago he was a fit senior cat.

That was another moment when I switched to autopilot. Even when deciding on an MRI examination. Do we need this to understand what he has? Yes. Is it inconvenient for everyone involved? Yes. Is it not exactly the cheapest diagnostics? Yes. Are we going to do it anyway? Yes. Because it's the only chance to find out what he has, so we can help him.

I didn't hesitate for a second and made an appointment for Flix to have an operation, scheduled for January 10th. Fortunately, I had just received my energetic clearing. I was very clear. I had no fear. Decisions had to be made. I made them.

I took him home as soon as he woke up from the anesthesia and was ready to be transported. He was in a grumbling state when they brought him to me. Max hissed at everyone when something didn't suit him or he wanted to vent his stress. Flix specialized in humming, a low growling sound. Although he could growl quite impressively; this definitely earned him some respect.

So we went home. We were very contemplative. What was going on here? Both cats have diseases that manifest themselves in the left ear? Even though the course of events was completely different. That was certainly something to think about. My left ear was itching too ...

As soon as we arrived at home, Flix jumped out of the cat carrier and, though it's hard to believe, staggered up the stairs; perhaps encouraged by the anesthesia, which still had a slight effect. I ran after him immediately to be able to catch him if necessary, which it was, because walking downstairs on his own was no longer possible for him.

I told Max what we had experienced and that Flix also had to have surgery on his left ear. Next week on January 10th.

Then I took a closer look at the day. January 10th was a very special day.

On January 10th, 2015, they both had come to our home. On this second anniversary, Flix would have an operation and it would be the last anniversary for Max in his forever home. Breathe in. Breathe out. Live in the here and now.

WHAT DOES THIS ALL MEAN?

Flix's diagnosis in addition to Max 'ear cancer and subsequent metastasis gave me a lot to think about. What kind of story is that and what are our roles? Why does Flix also develop a disease that manifests itself in the left ear? He had developed an illness several times when Max wasn't doing so well, but so far it had always been different.

Meanwhile, my left ear was itching as well, like back in August when we first learned about Max's cancer. The cancer in Max's ear must have been there much longer. Maybe he had it already when he came to us.

The questions for me were: Does Flix mirror Max's suffering, or do both mirror a situation of their humans, or is there perhaps no connection at all?

Were the two so closely connected that Flix couldn't help but literally lose his balance as soon as he realized that Max was facing his final days? Max was much more than his friend. He had played many roles for Flix:

Max, who had always protected him.

Max, who had taken care of him because he was so sad.

Max, who had always given him strength.

Max, who had always given him space, confidence, and trust.

Max, who had made sure that they would both be adopted by us.

Max, who had always assessed every situation and had made decisions for both of them.

Flix was no longer a youngster, and the operation on the middle ear was also a little more complex than removing tartar. So, I wanted to ensure the best possible recovery for him. This also included energetic support. Sylvia would go on a healing journey with him after his surgery.

In the meantime, Max had friends visiting. Animals must be able to say goodbye. It was important to me that people he knew and liked could say goodbye. Our dear friend Wally, for example, came to visit us. When she came, Max was trying out a built-in closet drawer in the bedroom for himself. He listened to her carefully; he knew exactly why she was there. It was very touching; for all of us.

SURGERY ON JANUARY 10th – AND THE ODYSSEY BEGINS

Taking away the food before midnight was one of the important steps in preparing Flix for his surgery. Fortunately, he had eaten well the past few days. He had even stolen food from Max ... who was probably sneakily happy because I assumed he had eaten something after all.

On the morning of January 10th, there was a lot of snow. Max went to the loggia to inspect his territory, sniff the snow and leave a paw print for his Cat Mum. Then he came back in and ran behind the sofa. That was one of Max's farewell messages that he wouldn't be here much longer. When I saw his paw print outside, I felt a sting in my heart. It was a very clear signal. I understood.

Nevertheless, I was very happy that he still enjoyed the snow so much! Euthanize him? Not a tomcat that still enjoys the snow.

Flix limited himself to looking at the snow from inside. He stopped at the doorstep, probably because he felt insecure on his little legs. He still faced a big program that day.

Flix had to spend the whole morning without food. Then I put him in the cat carrier. Since Max spent the morning behind the sofa in my study, I went back to him with Flix in the carrier so they could say goodbye.

At 12:30, I took Flix to the veterinary clinic. Leaving him there was one of the hardest things I had ever experienced. He didn't want to get out of his carrier, and when I put him on my arm, he clung to my jacket. For several minutes, we couldn't put him into the clinic carrier; even though we had already moved his blankets and toys there. I could feel his fear. I focused on giving him as much love as I could. Of course, I had explained to him beforehand via animal communication what was going to happen today.

Slowly he let go. The deeply sad, accusing look he gave me as I said goodbye was heartbreaking.

I drove home in tears, knowing full well that I had to be "normal" again at home with Max. I needed a lot of positive energy for Max, especially in order to explain to him that Flix would have to stay there overnight. This was because of the late surgery, the necessary monitoring overnight, and for the pain therapy.

The hours passed and, as always in such cases, I stared at my smartphone. I waited for it to finally ring, hoping that the veterinary clinic would tell me about a positive outcome. The operation was scheduled for 4:30 p.m.

When there was still no call after eight o'clock in the evening, I couldn't take it any longer and called them. They were just about to make the callbacks. Everything was OK so far, the operation went well, the tissue in the ear had been removed and the pathological exam was being done right now. The surgeon immediately pointed out to me that Flix's neurology could at first get either better or worse. Unfortunately, he was right about the latter. The next day the clinic called in the afternoon. Flix wasn't allowed to go home yet because he couldn't stand on his own and fell over to the right. In addition, he did not want to eat and had to be fed with a syringe. They wanted to wait for the next day, Thursday. He just needed more time.

I talked a lot with Max that evening, explaining to him that Flix had to stay in the clinic for another night, and that I very much hoped to be able to bring him home tomorrow. Max seemed to be listening attentively, but somehow he was already far away.

NAVIGATING WITH THE HEART

As so often in life, everything happens at once. What at first looks like sheer chaos then dissolves. Often it is only afterwards that you see how things all interacted, and why they dissolved the way they did and not differently. All in cosmic order. Just as the souls wanted it.

What a complicated situation: Flix was not doing well at the veterinary clinic and Max was also noticeably worse at home. He was about to say goodbye, that was obvious. He had been preparing his departure for weeks; that was clear to us. He had conserved his strength very well in the last few weeks, and ate just as much as he needed to maintain certain routines.

However, that changed in the week of Flix's surgery. Since Flix had gone to the veterinary clinic, Max ate next to nothing. He took his painkillers and a little of the recovery food. The week before, he had consciously enjoyed the midday sun in the living room. But now, he no longer did that either. He usually stayed behind the sofa in my study, or lay in his favorite cardboard box, or slept on his favorite blanket in Michael's study.

It was clear that these were his last days.

He drank a lot during this time. We had hoped he would do that earlier because of his kidney disease. For more than a year he had eyed the cat fountain rather skeptically, only to take a sip from the water bowl. Now the fountain was his favorite point of contact several times a day. He always took a few sips at a time. He didn't seem to have any difficulty swallowing.

Max had always been very clear in his decisions; he wasn't called "Sir Max" for nothing. That characteristic became more pronounced. "No, today I'll stay behind the sofa, even if you block me from doing it." On the evening before Flix's surgery, I blocked the sofa access because I didn't want Flix to hide behind the sofa; I might not have been able to get him out.

Max, one would assume, didn't have much strength left. Nevertheless, he could easily jump on the sofa, then leap from the corner of the wall to the back, and thus get to his favorite place. Cats ... "No, we're not going to the vet today. Period." Sir Max had spoken.

Of course, we have always dealt with the question of when the right time would be to help Max start the journey to cross the Rainbow Bridge. Whenever we had discussed this, or even if we had only thought about it, a signal came shortly afterwards that somehow seemed to say: "I'll go soon, but in my own way." Like enjoying the snow and leaving the paw print. If a day starts like this, it's not yet *the* day ...

I also increasingly felt that he wanted to be there for Flix, to help him. But Flix had to stay in the clinic longer than planned. What to do if Max's strength should no longer be sufficient and Flix's strength would also dwindle? Maybe the two could no longer say goodbye to each other?

We also discussed this with Max's vet, who has always stood by us very trustingly, but also very openly, through the whole time of Max's cancer treatment. She told us what to do to keep him relatively stable. But, she was also very clear when she stated: "We can no longer win the fight against cancer."

When we described the symptoms and signals to her, it was clear to her that Max was living the last few days of his life. It was Wednesday and we hoped that we could bring Flix home tomorrow. Then we could consider Max's release for Friday. We considered the situation, torn back and forth between Max's dwindling strength and Flix's slow recovery, which was contrary to expectations. One thing was clear: the two must see each other; as quickly as possible.

The next day, I visited Flix in the clinic, inspired by the thought that his spirits would be awakened again as soon as he saw me.

Flix was a picture of misery. There was no other way to describe it. He was huddled in his basket, and looked at me for a long time, as if far away. I took him out and just hugged him. Sending all my love straight to his heart for the next half hour. That's the time we had together. Even on the second day after surgery, he was still unable to stand. I had the bad feeling that he was going to give up right there and then.

How could it all fall apart like this? Should we have made Flix suffer so Max could leave earlier? Weighing one suffering against the other? And again the feeling was that Max wanted to decide for himself. And that Flix was mirroring Max.

I drove home from the veterinary clinic with tears in my eyes. I was too emotionally involved to speak to both of them myself. This was a clear case for Sylvia. I described the situation to her, that Flix was not doing well after the operation and that Max was getting increasingly weaker—and I was helplessly navigating between them.

She then spoke to both of them on the same evening, via an animal communication conference call, so to speak. As always, I was once again deeply impressed.

This was the result of the feline conference call:

———————

Dear Tamara,

I talked to Max. And at the same time with Flix.

Max's body feelings are shortness of breath and tightness in the chest. His body shuddering and being weak. He's so tired ... I feel this pressure in my ear and down the neck and on the lower jaw, very vaguely. It tingles, it feels numb inside and I feel nauseous. The legs are very weak, almost as if he were floating ... I feel a dizziness ... and a pressure on the left side of the head and behind the eye.

He says Flix can't stand because the one side of him is Max, who gave him support ... Flix feels that Max is "going away" ... therefore ... *"He can't take anything off me ... I'm so sorry ..."*

"But Flix will come home again ... I don't know if I can still wait ... Flix knows that ... That's why he lacks the strength ... my strength ... my half ... breaks away ... "

"Do you want to go?" "We won't decide that ... I want to sleep ..."

"Do you want help?" "There is no help ... I want to wait a little longer ... fly away when the time comes."

"Are you telling him that ... He shouldn't worry ... He should be strong ... If not here ... we'll see you there ... I'm sorry" ...

I then traveled with Max. Was with him on my empty beach somewhere in the universe. I prayed for him and did various healing processes. No matter where the path leads. I've seen him with wings. My white buffalo woman will accompany him. Thank you Max. You wonderful soul!

Then I talked to Flix. His body feelings are almost the same as Max's. Even the nausea, shortness of breath. Dizziness. Pressure on the left side. Head. Pulling in ear and neck, toward the jaw. Weak legs. Shuddering.

And fear. Yes, he is afraid that he can no longer be there for Max, that he has failed. *"My other half ..."* And somehow I have the feeling that he is not fighting, giving himself up to accompany Max.

I talk to him, tell him that Max wants him to be strong. Even if he can no longer be there for him. And I hope Flix understands! The soul is so important for healing.

I also traveled for Flix. And he kept turning and turning, his soul is completely unsteady. His world is collapsing right now. Yes, Max is the stronger one at the moment, despite everything.

I stopped his "turning" and first brought him back out of this unsteady vortex and went through various quantum healing processes. Yes, the balance is disturbed, the balance of the soul! I have a feeling it will take a little longer.

Be strong ... for Max. Live for him! All the life he can no longer live. For the both of you! This is what you can do for him!

I'll stay with him a while longer. He lies weakly on his side, takes short breaths. I caress him with long strokes across his body; until he calms down.

Thank you Flix, you wonderful soul!

Dear Tamara, everything that happens is out of our hands. The souls decide. I did everything I could. Now we have to wait and see.

All the best

Sylvia

I can't tell how many times I had to read this, because my eyes were so full of tears that I had to start over and over again. What wonderful souls they are. What an intimate bond that extends far beyond death. It gives me goose bumps. My heart overflowed with love and admiration.

Anything, I'll do anything to bring the two together. That's the least I can do right now.

The very next morning I called the veterinary clinic and explained the whole situation in a moving voice, including the results of the animal communication. They would discuss it. A short time later they called back and told me that under these circumstances they would give me Flix despite his poor condition. I went to the clinic in the early afternoon to take my beloved Flix home with me, along with eight medications. He was no longer lying in the cat basket; he was already sitting in it and looked at me for a long time.

He could stand again!

"We're going home to Max!" I told him. He even paid attention to some of the trip, but probably didn't have the energy to also comment on things.

When I got home, I put the cat carrier in the usual place and opened it. Lo and behold, Flix crawled out and then trotted over to Max behind the sofa with wobbly legs.

Tears. Joy. Love. Relief. Everything at once. My soul cats!

A heart was shaved on Flix's chest when he came out of the clinic. They had reached the middle ear from an incision in the neck. And, his head was tilted to the side because of the vestibular syndrome.

Now it was time to prepare Flix's medication for the evening, and I quickly familiarized myself with feeding by syringe. He had been fed like this for the past few days, since he didn't eat on his own. We were able to get this done. Flix could be fed with the syringe without any problems.

Both cats relaxed visibly. To see Flix at home and compare it with how I experienced him the day before—a picture of misery at the clinic—these were two different worlds. And Max relaxed too when Flix came home. He was visibly relieved that he didn't have to leave this life without being able to say goodbye to his beloved Flix.

Max's Journey to Rainbowland

Bringing Flix home from the clinic had been the right thing to do. Clearly "divine right timing." Max was able to prepare himself for his actual mission. And, that was leaving this life, leaving his sick and now aching body to cross the Rainbow Bridge and to continue his journey as a soul.

On Saturday he was behind the sofa in my study most of the time. He just changed position. Once he looked ahead and then back again. He only came out briefly to drink water from the fountain. Then he was back in his favorite hideout. He hadn't touched his food today either. It was one of the last days, that much was clear.

In the early evening he had switched places. He went into Michael's study and lay down in his box of favorite blankets. Flix was in the room too. I came over and talked to him and stroked his silky, still shiny fur.

I asked him if I should give him his recovery food and pain killer. He looked at me indifferently, as if he were already far away. I went into the kitchen and prepared his syringe.

When I came back, he was lying there, his position unchanged, and looking at me. I gave him a little sip. A little burp followed.

But then he turned to the other, right side of his body. That was different than usual. I knew instinctively that the time had come to say goodbye, and that I wanted to do everything for him to accompany him in the best possible way.

He had chosen to come to Michael's room so that Flix and I could accompany him when his soul left his body, when he was about to cross the Rainbow Bridge. It wasn't until much later that I realized the trust he had in me, and how much love he gave me right there. That he invited me to accompany him on his last journey on Earth before transitioning. That still fills me with deep gratitude and unconditional love.

Instinctively, as if guided by a higher power, I began to sing what my heart wanted to sing. Max knew the song; I had sung it for him when I held him in my arms before his ear surgery in the clinic until he was taken away by the vets.

This song had always created a very close bond between us. Souls understand each other through symbols, colors, and sounds. Language is often not the right medium. The song gave him confidence and strength for the path that lay ahead. I sang for him, gently stroked his back and his head to give him protection and space, and not to constrict him.

I stroked his beautiful fur. Tears ran down my cheeks. My tears came from my deep love for Max. With what greatness, with what consideration, and with what decisiveness he had determined his own transition. And, he still had the strength to make Flix strong so that he could go on living without him.

My tears also came from a deeply felt relief that Max's release had now come. He had fought so bravely against cancer until he realized, earlier than we did, that this battle was not to be won. He had just as consistently taken care of his departure from this life and prepared for it.

And my tears were also a testament to the happiness and gratitude I felt, that I was allowed to live with Max for two years and four days. That he chose us as the last home in this life and adopted us.

And of course my tears came from deep sadness that he would never again walk through the apartment with almost military precision. Never touch my legs again. That he would never sunbathe at noon and would never again sit on my lap to keep me from work. Or to be there while I was eating, allowing me to hold and feel him.

After a few moments, Max was gone. One last deep breath, then his soul left this body and made its way over the Rainbow Bridge.

I sat in silence next to his body for minutes, just kept singing. Then I closed his eyes and covered him with the rest of the blanket. And kept singing to accompany his soul on his journey with a lot of love. May Max's soul arrive safely in Rainbowland and be greeted warmly by many animal souls. He would take over the reins there soon enough. I had no doubt about that.

The whole time Flix sat less than 6 feet from us and watched everything. Quietly. He was also a very wise cat.

JUST KEEP KEEPING ON

After we had all cried our eyes out, it was time to organize. We had already discussed in advance that we wanted an individual cremation for Max, so that he could then come home again.

I called a local animal cremation service that same evening with a trembling voice. I had never consciously thought about this myself, but my soul led me there. A woman from the CKD group, who lives not far away and had to let her cat go a few weeks earlier, recommended a particular cremation service. Then I saw the flyer of exactly that service at Max's vet. It had hung there for weeks, but I only became aware of it a few days before Max died.

The next morning, we took Max there. In his favorite blanket, with his toys. Choosing the urn was overwhelming at that moment. It should be simple, classy, elegant. And not look like an urn. I didn't see anything like that there. We decided to look for it ourselves. No problem for the mortician. Back home, we found something online. Something elegant, cat-shaped. In black.

Well, you are probably wondering what my experience was like the next few days, right after Max's death. I only did what I had to do, my focus was now entirely on Flix and his recovery. Since he had to take a lot of medication, his care not only required a lot of love, but also time, skill, and a great deal of trickery when it came to medication.

After all, we wanted to create a great impression for the neurologist on the following Thursday, with Flix in good shape. He made more progress every day. Small, steady steps in the right direction. And along with this, of course, we realized that we were all very sad because we missed our Max so much. For Flix, Max was the great support in his life. During his last hours, Flix convinced Max about his confidence in being able to go on living and get well again without him. That meant Max could leave in peace. Flix would find his way.

In fact, Flix was brave, very aware, and very focused. After a few days, he tried really hard to get his treats out of the activity feeder himself. At first he couldn't position his legs correctly; they landed right next to the treat. But, he learned to do it again quickly. Most interestingly: as soon as he was busy with something—eating, drinking or grabbing treats—his head was straight again. However, if he walked or ran normally, his head was tilted. Somehow that looked very cute on him!

Thursday came with the follow-up examination at the veterinary hospital. Neurologist visit and taking his blood pressure were on the program. He didn't give them any trouble while they were taking his blood pressure; it was in the normal range, controlled with the blood pressure medication he received. We would keep using this drug that he had been on since the surgery, but now administer half the dosage. Amodip[1] would become his long-term medication.

All neurological tests were satisfactory. In particular, the videos that I had already shared by email before the appointment were very helpful for the vet to observe Flix in his familiar surroundings. He also thought it was absolutely right to take Flix home and allow him and Max to say goodbye. "Animals also have to say goodbye to each other," he said. This vet had been only called in when Flix was in the clinic, precisely because Flix had not initially recovered well. We now knew that had to do with Max's departure.

After this appointment was over and we arrived back home, I was able to slowly release my tension. We were really on the right track with Flix. That was very important to me. He had cleared all the hurdles that had to be cleared in this very short time. Now, most of all, he would need time to heal. A lot of time, a lot of care, and even more love. Of course, he would get all of this to enable him to have a good cat life again.

---

1. Amlodipine (brand names: Norvasc®, Amodip®, Copalia®, Katerzia®) is a calcium channel blocker used for treating high blood pressure, most commonly in cats, in order to prevent damage to the kidneys, eyes, and brain.
Its use in cats and dogs to treat high blood pressure is "off label" or "extra label".
Source: https://vcahospitals.com/know-your-pet/amlodipine-besylate

MOURNING OR LIFE WITHOUT MAX

Only after visiting the vet with Flix on January 19th did I realize what had happened in such a condensed way in these few days. Only now could I allow myself to embrace the grief, the deep sadness that Max was no longer with us. Accept his death internally. Finally let the tears flow freely.

Max appeared to me in a dream that night. He admonished me to give myself and my soul space and time to deal with everything that had happened. And, he let me know that he was fine, that everything was fine now.

He was right. As I suspected, Max was still busy looking after me. As was true during his life, he had often cared more about me than about himself.

The evening he died and for the next few weeks, I lit a white candle for him outside on the loggia. It was a refuge for me. To spend time with him and our memories, to feel him. I often sat outside, even when it was cold, to hang out with him. To really feel and process all that had happened. And the intensity of it! He had only been with us for two years and four days—physically.

Almost four weeks after Max's death, I consciously tried to contact him, as I had learned from Sylvia. Lo and behold, it worked! There was an intimate connection, as if he were very close, just not in his body anymore. But around me, Max was everywhere, as was his energy. Wonderful. So beautiful. It cannot be put into words. Once again, this was one of the experiences when I found the human language to be very limiting.

In late March, I was in Scotland for a week attending the fourth and final module of my spiritual leadership seminar. At the end of the seminar, we had a closing ritual where we were all energized by our teacher. I had given my little photo book to one of the participants, my dear friend Jayne, who has dogs and cats herself. It described the year 2016 with Max and Flix in pictures. In the morning, she told me that she would like to put the little book showing Max on the cover on the altar in the middle of our circle, so that Max and Flix could be here with us. What a wonderful idea—but also one that brought tears to my eyes at the same time.

Boom. A wave of deep love with incredible intensity came over me. I then sat in my seat during this ritual; tears just ran silently down my cheeks. Max was there. He was here with me. He sensed that this was a very important milestone for me. There he was and he said, "Luckily, Jayne thought of including me. You were probably afraid of your own feelings again."

He was here. Max was here. He was so present. So intense. Right among us.

How right he was! It was exactly like that! Because I was haunted by my emotions and didn't want to accept them. My heart had so much more to say than my words ever could. So I cried more tears to express all that I couldn't some other way.

Max let me know that this experience was important to me. I needed to trust, to trust more. Trust the process—my process—the universe. And that everything would be fine. That's why he was here with me, after all.

When it was my turn in the ritual, I shed even more tears. Tears of love, happiness, relief, and gratitude. After the ritual was over, our teacher Peggy came up to me and said: "Max was all around you."

Energy. It's all energy. Learning to feel, sense, and work with energies is the most wonderful thing. And it's all physics. Actually nothing mysterious, even though it isn't easy to understand.

Lendrick Lodge, where the seminar was held, has another point of relevance, a feline one. And, the feline's name is Sam. Scottish Sam. The tomcat of Lendrick Lodge. He's Stevie's cat. Stevie is the gardener there; he takes care of everything around the lodge. He lives in a smaller "log cabin" on the premises. With Sam.

Sam is a very special personality. He is very busy with his vast territory. He doesn't accept people walking up to him. No, *he* walks up to people. To selected people. If his tight schedule permits. I was one of the very few people

Sam honored with a visit. He allowed me to watch him clean himself and we talked. He would sometimes jump from behind, over my shoulder onto my lap, when I was sitting outside with other participants. He stayed on my lap for a short time, and then continued to pursue his mission, strengthened after I had stroked him.

You are probably wondering why I am telling you all this. Because Sam's owner, Stevie, heard about Max's passing and also about my plan to write a book. This book with the title "Soul Cats." Already at the end of January, when I was there for a weekend, I had the idea. He told me that I should read the book *Living With The Lama*,[1] that it would surely inspire me.

I came home at the end of January, ordered that book, devoured it, and one thing was clear: animal communication, which had opened up a completely different dimension, would play a special role in my book. In addition, this wonderful book also had a few passages in which the protagonist, Mrs. Fifi Greywhiskers, an elderly Siamese cat, explains how telepathy works and exactly how one makes telepathic "local and long-distance calls:"

Let me tell you something; we do not speak English, nor French, nor Chinese, not so far as the sounds go, but we understand those languages. We converse by thought. We "understand" by thought. So did humans before…yes, before they were treacherous to the animal world and so LOST the power of thought reading! We do not use "reason" (as such) we have no frontal lobes; we KNOW by intuition. The answers "come" to us without having to work out the problems. Humans use telephone in order to speak over a distance. They have to know a "number." We cats, when we know the "number" of the cat we desire to speak, can send our messages over hundreds of miles by telepathy. Very rarely can humans understand our telepathic messages.

Humans thoughts are uncontrolled and radiate everywhere. Only people like my Guv can control the radiation and spread of their thoughts so as not to "jam" all others. The Guv told Miss Ku and me that humans conversed by telepathy many many years ago, but they abused the power badly and so lost it. This, the Guv says, is

1. T. Lobsang Rampa: *Living With The Lama*, ISBN 9 781892 062390

the meaning of the Tower of Babel. Like us, many humans formerly used vocal speech for private talk within a group, and telepathy for long distance and group use. Now, of course, humans, or most of them, use vocal speech only.

Excerpt from *Living With The Lama,* by T. Lobsang Rampa, page 76 and page 92.

HEART FORM, SOUL FORM

What a great surprise I found cleaning the cat litter box. Flix left me a slightly belated Valentine's greeting! A peed heart! Max had done this too after each successful surgery.

Slowly, the thought of living a life without Max became reality. Although "without Max" isn't entirely accurate. I feel Max very often. I frequently feel his energy. It feels good, makes my heart beat faster and fills me with deep joy. It makes me so happy, on the inside, even if I miss him physically. It's as if he wanted to say: "I am here. All is well."

Flix obviously saw it that way too. Max was often with us. And everything was fine.

And, Flix got better every day, with Max by his side—Max in soul form. In this way, the two spent many sunny afternoons in the living room.

One month after Max's death, I informed the animal health practitioner who had also drawn up a therapy plan for Max. He had sent me a text that really touched me:

> *The Beginning of the Rainbow*
> *Exactly where the sky is most beautiful, there is a place*
> *where the beginning of the rainbow can be found—Ananghal.*
> *When an animal's time here on Earth is over, it*
> *leaves for Ananghal.*

*All the animals that were sick and old get their strength and
health back. All who were injured or crippled will
be whole again.
Animals may stay in Ananghal until their human
has said goodbye to them for good.
Only then do they set off. It is their last journey on
Earth.
Their path leads them over the rainbow, into the land of light
and of love ... there, where we are all at home.
(Avana Eder)*

HE WANTED TO WAKE US AGAIN
IN THE MORNINGS

Flix had been somewhat overshadowed by Max. For one, Max was almost twice as tall. Max was also just a more extroverted cat. And of course, Max was undisputedly the Boss Cat.

In addition, Max's CKD had required a certain level of attention, as did the two dental restorations long before we found out about his cancer. Fortunately, Flix didn't need this level of attention and care until recently. His kidneys were relatively healthy for his age, and we had his vomiting under control through rebuilding of his intestinal flora.

After we had successfully survived the first days and weeks following Flix's surgery, and he was able to eat by himself again and go to the litter box, it was now a matter of helping him find his way back into his cat life. He had to learn many things anew. Things that seem quite normal, such as locating, grabbing, and eating treats. Walking over objects. Jumping on the sofa. Going upstairs. Since he clearly had a tilt to his head, we naturally wanted to try to improve that.

In the weeks after Max's death, Flix surpassed all expectations, seemed healthier than ever before. He developed strength, self-esteem, and a much deeper trust. I have to emphasize again and again, how many "hurdles" he had to clear at the same time.

On the one hand, he had to deal with the loss of Max's physical presence. Then he had to recover from the physical strains of his surgery and its after-effects. He was one of the few cases where the neurological system deteriorates. His neurological system now had to be supported, strengthened, and trained, so he could fight his way back to his cat life, step by step. It was our guiding principle that everything should go at Flix's pace. Under no circumstances should he feel stressed because we had unrealistic expectations of him. And, that meant that we supported him in what he wanted to do himself. That we asked him to play, but we ignored his tilted head, except that we often massaged his neck, because we knew that this symptom might possibly remain.

The most important requirement for Flix's mental and physical recovery was that he could see Max again, at least for 24 hours. They could say goodbye to each other, say everything that still had to be said. Flix was calm when Max's soul left his body. In retrospect, I cannot stress enough how important it is for animals to be able to say goodbye to each other. And, that they are given this opportunity whenever possible.

He no longer had his loyal friend, protector, and savior Max by his side. He had to be strong by himself. Take everything in his own paws that Max had done for him before. It was he who had to make decisions alone now. He grew into this role just fine. And now, Flix had the undivided attention of his staff.

Again and again, I encouraged him to grab treats and eat them. At first he had difficulty locating them because his head was tilted and his world therefore looked slanted as well. He had to completely relearn and modify familiar, routine patterns of movements.

Imagine for a moment that you see everything on a slanted plane. Furthermore, imagine that you have to re-coordinate your limbs appropriately to do everyday things like running straight, turning corners, going to the bathroom, putting food in your mouth, drinking water, and climbing stairs.

We made the first progress with treats in the activity feeder. This provided seven different fields that train different senses. Little by little, he learned again to grab his beloved treats, to take them out, and to eat them. You could see how much he enjoyed it when he mastered something and he could reward himself with a treat. And I praised my beloved Flix a lot. You can say I showered him with praise. Every time and immediately after he had grabbed the treat.

Flix was extremely self-motivated at all times to fight his way back into his cat life. We could only help. I never saw him sad, depressed, or disillusioned. Never. Even though he faced great physical limitations.

There's no doubt that he trained himself. He wanted to be able to do everything again. Wanted to have a joyful life again, playing with treats and keeping himself busy.

After one week, he could eat his moist food without any assistance. Here, too, it was funny at first to see him approach the feeding bowl because, due to the tilted posture of his head, he approached the bowl in a slightly circular fashion from the outside, and ate his food from the outside in.

It was very similar with drinking. He sat in front of the water bowl and wondered how he should do it now. Here, too, he approached it in a circle from the outside in. Sipping water from the outer, rear edge has remained the preferred practice to this day.

In the first few weeks, climbing stairs was out of the question. We were overjoyed that he could walk straight and navigate around corners.

Then he slowly started to stand by the stairs. Little by little, he learned how to climb stairs. He wanted to wake us up again in the morning. It was February, almost eight weeks after his surgery, when he learned again to walk up the stairs. Step by step. One paw on one step, then pull the others up. Then the next step. And so on until he had reached the top. What a milestone! Going down was harder. That took a lot more time. So, we always carried him down during this phase. This incredible display of trust from this wonderful cat still gives me goose bumps.

Almost three months after the operation, he was able to walk down the stairs by himself. We practiced that with him. Encouraged him when he signaled that he wanted to practice. Took breaks on the stairs, always being by his side. He leaned against the wall for additional support.

Before he was able to go down the stairs, he learned to jump onto the sofa. He kept walking past the sofa, looking up longingly, but somehow he didn't know how to do it. At first, we always picked him up. But he wanted to be able to do it again himself. He stood in front of it and thought about it. He's a very contemplative personality anyway. Something in me told me that he was brooding too much about it, that he would need a little more self-confidence and courage.

An idea came to me during my energy clearing work, like the clearing of energetic blockages in the auric field, as well as clearing of karmic blockages, which I had learned as well. I tuned into Flix's feelings, connected with his Higher Self, and manifested for him that he had all the power, strength, and ability to jump onto the sofa. I cleared the existing energetic blockages that stood in the way.

He was looking at me from a few feet away when I was doing this energetic clearing work. He immediately understood what I had initiated for him. Half an hour later, Flix jumped up on the sofa. What an indescribable joy for cat and Cat Mum! Tears of joy without end!

From that moment on, something fundamentally changed. He was so happy with himself that he could now do almost everything again that was important to him. Much of it had to do with his ability to interact with his humans.

Soon after mastering the sofa, came accomplishing the stairs. He could now resume his routine, which was making sure that the staff went to sleep and would get up again the next morning.

Next, we started working on the cat trees in a playful way. There was the large cat tree, the ceiling clamping unit, and a smaller one in the living room; as well as another smaller one in my study and a partial cupboard cat tree in Michael's study.

At first I made the mistake of putting him on the first or second level of the big cat tree. I figured that he should be able to climb up and down from there. But this was not so. He didn't climb up himself; he clearly didn't know how to get up. He became very stressed trying to come down. He jumped down from much too great a height and, as expected, landed badly. I didn't learn until later that it was very important that he could climb up himself. So, we shifted our efforts to the smaller cat tree, the bottom step of which was significantly lower.

From this level, he had the opportunity to stretch and climb into his cave. He did that in April, a little more than three months after the surgery. Lured with treats, he learned to jump to the first level. When he felt safe doing it, more treats followed at the entrance to the cave. For many days they were just lying there. Then he started pulling them down with his paw. Clever cat.

In early May, the time had come. When he was able to climb back into his cave for the first time, I cried with joy, just as I did when he took the first steps up the stairs and the first jump onto the sofa.

It took all of his senses and all his strength as he heaved himself into the cave. But here too, he showed strong will, determination, and motivation. And an indescribable joy when he succeeded in something, when he mastered a challenge with bravura.

FROM AN ENERGETIC VIEWPOINT

Energy became my passion; a central topic in my life. For myself, for our cats, and for my work. In addition to my job as an analyst and researcher, I educated myself broadly in the areas of energy, energy fields, aura and soul work.

Among other things, I learned how to read the so-called Akashic Records, the energetic data record of one's soul, and how to create your own soul blueprint based on it. I took a training course, passed the exam and was then, after the course in 2017, able to call myself "Advanced Soul Realignment Practitioner." I started offering this service to clients, with great joy and success. It's such a wonderful and fulfilling job, which I still enjoy today—every single reading and clearing. It is wonderful to give people insights and new perspectives that they haven't had before; to pave new paths for them that they previously thought impossible.

For example, imagine you have big plans, be it career advancement, starting your own business, writing a book, or moving to another country. But, at the same time, you have various limiting beliefs and mind patterns that you are constantly, but unconsciously, thinking. "It won't work anyway." "Only other people can do that." "I probably don't deserve it." What do you think these will do to you and your plans? Exactly, these beliefs stand in your way like roadblocks and prevent progress. You can metaphorically get out of the car and clear away all the roadblocks, then get back in and reach your destination. Or, you can turn the car around and forget about your plans. These beliefs are often deeply anchored in us over generations, or perhaps we have adopted them ourselves. Unfortunately, you can't just "talk them away" so easily. The limiting energy of these thought patterns remains in your energy field until they are cleared. When you clear them, your energy frequency increases significantly, new perspectives open up, your intuition can now get through to you without any blockages, and you can implement your plans much sooner.

Over time, I developed these techniques further and tailored them specifically to people who are at a professional crossroads. Because precisely at this point, it is incredibly important to understand on a deeper level where hidden strengths and energetic riches lie. Figuring out how to make them shine and resound allows them to serve their purpose in the here and now. At the time, I didn't know how much of this I would need later for myself as well.

I also learned energetic clearing methods to cleanse the human and animal energy field, the aura, of everything that does not belong there and literally stands in your way like a roadblock.

How does that fit together, you ask yourself? Being an analyst on the one hand, very data and fact-oriented, seeking to combine with something spiritual that has not been proven? I'll try to explain it in simple terms. And scientifically.

Most of us learned in school to understand the world based on theories of Isaac Newton. This world model from the 17th Century is based on the theory of gravity and a dualistic natural philosophy: there is matter and there is energy.

With regard to humans and animals, this means that the body is understood as a precise and highly complex mechanism in which organs, blood and lymphatic systems, enzymes, membranes and receptors, as well as hormonal balances, interact in a finely tuned manner. Additional cycles, such as an energy cycle that is invisible to humans, are not part of this model. The highly specialized and very organ-specific therapeutic approaches of conventional medicine also are based on this.

On the other hand, there is Albert Einstein's model, which leads us to quantum physics, having long replaced Newton's model in science. Max Planck discovered the quantum actions at the turn of the 20th Century, and

Albert Einstein published his theory of relativity. Physics is still concerned with these topics today.

So what does the world look like from the perspective of the latest scientific knowledge based on quantum physics? The key point is that solid matter doesn't exist in essence. Rather, everything is energy. And this energy, which includes everything, comes in different vibrations and frequencies. As a result, we perceive certain energies as solid, that is, as "matter," and other energies as ethereal, having no tangible form. But it's all energy. The differences in perception are due to different vibrations and frequencies.

Albert Einstein sums it up: "As far as matter is concerned, we were all wrong. What we called matter is energy, the vibrations of which were slowed so much that it becomes perceptible to the senses. There is no matter." Or Hans-Peter Dürr, one of the most famous quantum physicists of the modern era, said in the 1990s: "In principle, matter is not matter. That's why I already indicated: I've worked for fifty years on matter that doesn't even exist ... There are only relational structures, there are no objects."

That's the beauty of science. It's always the latest findings that apply. As soon as new, better insights are gained, they replace the old ones. It doesn't always happen readily. Not even with quantum physics. The scientists themselves had to overcome a number of challenges in dealing with what they had discovered. When Einstein presented his Theory of Relativity, a colleague came along and said: "You know, Professor, it all sounds very adventurous. I prefer to trust my common sense. I just believe what I see." Einstein smiled and said: "Then please come up to the front and put your common sense on the table so I can see it."

If you look at today's modern conventional medicine, you quickly see that this basic idea still prevails. What is not seen or felt in the blood count, ultrasound or X-ray image does not exist—for the time being.

Vibrational medicine, which is energetic, holistic medicine, is slowly gaining ground. For years there have been interesting studies of the structure of energy fields of living beings. And, there are many studies that clearly demonstrate energy fields. Modern cameras can depict the aura of living things. According to physics laws, different colors represent different energy frequencies.

This energetic approach combines Eastern teachings that are several thousand years old and have an energetic perspective, for example traditional

Chinese medicine or yoga, with Western knowledge of conventional medicine.

Every emotion, every thought has a certain energy frequency. So does every experience we have. For example, a shock or an accident leads to trauma, creating energy with a very low frequency. In a state of shock, an energetic blockage forms that attaches to the chakra to which the underlying emotion corresponds. Love and joy have the highest energy frequency. The higher the energy frequency of a living being, the fewer blockages there are in the aura, and the better the being feels.

Getting this blocked energy to flow freely is the task of those who deal with, and have dedicated themselves to, energy healing. And, that's exactly what fascinated me. In my parallel training with Toby Alexander, I focused on what is known as aura clearing. Aura clearing is about removing energetic blockages that can adhere to any of the body's seven chakras, as well as to the eight morphogenetic chakras that surround the body.

Energetic blockages that attach to chakras and then inhibit the flow of vital life energy through them, not only have behavior-related effects, but are sooner or later often revealed in physical symptoms. Which chakras the blockages are attached to points to the cause that needs to be addressed.

Back to our cats. They came to us with some baggage from their previous lives. Disappointments, grief, fear, worries, especially lack of trust in Flix's case. These are mostly the issues which animals adopted from shelters bring with them to their new home. Some of them are even downright traumatized, especially when they come from shelters that practice euthanasia after long stays, or if they have been mistreated. But, even animals that have lost a loved one and do not understand the situation because no one explains it to them are traumatized, and accordingly come with a lot of baggage from an energetic point of view.

It's not true that time heals all wounds. Of course, the animals relax and they regain confidence, but the energetic cause for the problem still remains. That is why there are situations in which such an animal "all of the sudden freaks out" and, depending on the effects, is often returned to the animal shelter. Sadly, they are returned with even more emotional wounds, with even more energetic blockages.

The background to such situations is as follows: In a shock situation, in a traumatic situation, when time seems to stand still, large energetic blockages arise that attach themselves to a corresponding chakra. For example, "feeling betrayed" attaches itself to the heart chakra, while struggles for survival attach to the root chakra. These energies form so-called "buttons." You probably know the expression that some people know how to push your "buttons." Well, these buttons have to be installed beforehand, of course; otherwise there is nothing to push.

So, if an identical or similar situation occurs again, this chakra button is, as it were, pushed. The body remembers the program that ran the last time and starts it up again. This is not ideal, neither in people nor in our animals. It is not uncommon for such situations to be dangerous, and it makes no difference whether it is animals or people. The principle of energetic blockages, how they are formed and how they can be cleared is the same.

These situations arise for one reason: because the causal energetic "button" was not removed This is why I am so fascinated by energy, and why it's so fulfilling to do energy healing. It is so beneficial, transforming, often life changing. For humans and animals.

The animals are grateful to be heard and to be able to let go of these stressful experiences. Animals are more sensitive than most people when it comes to energy. Working with animals, you will immediately feel when you are energetically connecting with your Higher Self. But here is what's essential in working with all living beings: You always ask for permission. No energetic work without permission. Animals are grateful to receive help in this way.

I carried out the first aura clearing with Flix sitting on my lap. When I got to the heart chakra and cleared it from its blockages, he sighed and I could hear a gentle "plop." It was so beautiful to feel how a great burden was literally lifted from him, and how his heart was now much, much lighter. Blockages of the heart chakra include the emotions of being abandoned, experiencing rejection, not being able to love yourself, and many more.

Since then, these aura clearings have become routine. Everything that exists as blockages in the energy field is permanently cleared with this technique at the quantum level—and that means it's transmuted into nothing, into no-thing. The tricky thing is that you can get blockages again. It is the same with humans and animals.

Everything, from an energetic point of view that cannot simply flow through us, leads to energy affixing itself; this can cause a chakra to close up, and inhibit the flow of vital life force energy. For cats, it happens very quickly: An argument with your cat buddy, for whatever reason, can cause it. A stressful vet visit. Or Cat Mum leaving, bringing up the feeling of rejection or fear of loss, which settles in the heart chakra.

Flix is a cat who analyzes a lot, thinks about things, and rechecks things again and again. At the same time, he's highly sensitive. So, he worries a lot and often. No wonder that with him, it's mostly the second chakra where something needs to be cleared. This also explains why his kidneys are not the best, since they are energetically connected to the second chakra. Fear, worries, and anxiety create blockages that attach to the second chakra. This chakra is also responsible for the ability to manifest, or put something into action. Thus, you can see how important it is to basically "clear the fear."

The energy clearing approach had its uses with both cats and later also with Howy (you can look forward to Howy!), just as conventional medicine and the naturopathic paths did.

I don't want to praise one thing or criticize another. On the contrary: every form of therapy has its place. Often you have to try and try different things until you have found the right approach for your case. That was always my motto, and that's exactly how I apply it to myself and my cats. Of course, you need intensive medical care if pancreatitis is acute or if a tumor in the ear has to be operated on. I wouldn't want to miss out on the sophisticated diagnostic methods of conventional medicine either. No question about it. We have used them again and again with all cats and I will continue to do so.

However, you are also well advised if you follow a more holistic approach, especially if you want to alleviate chronic illnesses in the long term, or when a spiritual healing as just described is important. Above all, I want one thing: mutual respect and an integrative approach. It doesn't help anyone when veterinarians rail against alternative practitioners and vice versa; often both dismiss energetic work as complete nonsense. This is usually because they have not dealt with the topic and have no experience with it.

As an analyst, I am very clear on this point: Everyone can have their opinion, but should always communicate it as their own opinion and not as facts.

Hence my request to you: Always look carefully, do not let anyone talk you into believing ideologies without examining them for yourself. If you believe in some ideologies, or just don't know enough about a topic, buy a book, read it, do your research before you simply dismiss a potentially promising method with "I don't believe in something like that." And, there's a lot of good information available on the internet. But also a lot of nonsense. Always look carefully at the sources of the claims made.

So, I trained as an aura clearing practitioner, and in 2019, I became an Advanced Auric Clearing Practitioner. In 2020, I finally learned to train other practitioners in this field and became one of Toby's Licensed Certified Advanced Auric Clearing Master Healers. At the same time, I also learned karma clearing and became a practitioner.

Why do I write so much about this in a cat book? Well, it's a book about soul cats. Here everything goes a little further and deeper. Quite simply, because the lives of our cats are inextricably linked to my own personal development, and because what I have learned has very positively influenced the lives of Howy and Flix. And our human lives too.

Unfortunately, I didn't know enough about energy healing when Max needed it. However, Sylvia had worked energetically with both cats, so these methods also benefited Max. I only regret that I wasn't able to treat him myself when he was struck by cancer.

I mentioned the example of how I was able to help Flix jump back on the sofa. His fear stood in the way. Whenever he stood in front of the sofa, fear came up again. He stood in front of it and couldn't do it. Because fear dominated him, and not his conviction that he could do it. He oriented himself on what he did *not* want, what he had to overcome. He wasn't focusing on *what* he wanted. A basic problem that most people also have, collectively and individually.

As soon as this fear, which is energy with a low frequency, is cleared, your own energy rises and you can focus more easily on what you actually want to achieve. And that is the art of doing things successfully. Well, having learned all of this, I used aura and karma clearing a lot on myself before I started offering this service to humans and animals.

FLIX'S VIEW OF THINGS

Now a few months had passed without Max. Flix had recovered according to his circumstances. He lived a real cat life again, which he had fought back into with a lot of concentration, will power, and mental strength. Of course we supported him always. But, it would never have worked out so well without his will to fight his way back into his life.

Sure, he couldn't climb up on the big cat tree anymore. He couldn't manage the height between the individual levels anymore. He couldn't climb up on the cabinet either. He used to enjoy doing both. Still, I didn't get the impression that he was unhappy about it. At least he didn't show it. Rather, it seemed that he was enjoying whatever he could do once more. Now that it was warm again, he could enjoy the sun on the loggia and the balcony and let the wind caress his face.

However, he no longer had a four-legged friend in this world. He was alone with his staff. Somehow he seemed to enjoy the undivided attention; only, would it stay that way or would he get bored just being with humans?

We wanted to provide a home for another cat from the animal shelter, but not against Flix's will. Once again, it was time for professional animal communication with Sylvia. Although I had conducted the animal conversations for "regular life at home" myself, at this point I wanted a neutral point of view.

A few excerpts from Sylvia:

Flix shows me the world in slanted view when I look through his eyes and he also says *"The world has gotten slanted."* Yes, that's how he sees it. And since then he has had to concentrate incredibly hard, he tells me. But he doesn't see it as a burden, but as a challenge. Your praise in particular spurs him on and he enjoys your increased attention. He shows me your living room and how he wants to climb the cat tree. Slowly, thinking. And nearby, Max is crouching on the wooden floor as a matter of course and observing him *"as always."* There is nothing special about him being there because he is always there, Flix tells me. Just quietly watching.

Flix's hind legs can't bear the weight, I can feel his muscles in his thighs and lower legs on the left side because he keeps trying to balance here. *"The slanted thing."* Yes, he is proud of himself and of thinking, concentrating, and mastering difficult tasks. Push yourself like this and be praised afterwards. Wow. *"That is sooo great!"* And totally lifts him up. He loves being close to you and I see him with comfortably closed eyes on your arm. He loves the conversation and your voice and the gentle air outside on the balcony that caresses his fur. Flix is so incredibly content. I wish a lot of people had that feeling. It's called gratitude for all that is. A wonderful feeling of inner peace and serenity.

Would he like to have a feline friend by his side again or would he rather stay alone with us? If so, what should he or she be like?

Flix misses *"nothing."* Everything is wonderful and good and he is incredibly happy with everything that is.

I ask Flix if he misses a friend by his side and he thinks about it. *"Hmm … not necessarily. Well, not yet."* Or rather, he hasn't given it any thought, but since I ask him like that, he'd find it incredibly exciting, yes. But the cat would have to be kind and gentle and not take advantage of his *"weakness"* or be rude and push himself ahead. Just a gentle soul like himself *"and if he needs help …"* Flix would find it exciting to observe and interact.

But as I said: It would have to be a *"very special cat."*

As always, it is very emotional when an animal communication arrives in the inbox. You can't get to it quickly enough and then you read it again and again and again ... because so many tears well up. Tears of joy, of emotion and love, of infinite love for this best of all black and white tomcats.

I was so proud of Flix! I was able to experience anew every day how much he had grown in the face of his challenges. Still, hearing from his own mouth how he saw his development over the past few months was a particularly rewarding experience!

The assignment was clear: when a new cat comes along, he or she has to be something very special, a gentle and wise soul who won't take advantage of his situation.

A few days later in May, I went to attend my third module on animal communication. Talking to departed and missing animals was on the program. I had already connected with Max after his death, but I wanted to learn to do it "properly."

But first we should talk about how Flix got his senior cat tree and how it changed his world, clearly improving it!

SENIOR CAT TREE FOR FLIX

Soon I realized that the little cat tree helped Flix, but also obstructed him, as the area on the levels was too small for him to sit down or turn around. So we Googled to see what was available.

Indeed, there was such a thing as a senior cat tree. Two models were offered. Both models had much wider areas and either a staircase or two little steps to get from the ground to the first and second levels. Of course, the tree was ordered—the one with the little steps—and immediately assembled once it arrived. It was the beginning of May when the new cat tree was introduced.

What a blessing for Flix and his development! He followed the assembly with interest. When the new cat tree was in place—the old one went to the Mainz Animal Shelter—he got busy with it straight away. He sat down in front of it and thought about how he could get to the first level. It never occurred to him to take the specially designated steps. "Well, I'm not that old and sick," he seemed to be saying. He managed to jump to the first level in one go. Since he now had a lot more space, he could eat the reward treats there without any difficulty. The two steps that led to the upper level were great for placing more treats that he could look for, find and eat.

What a joy for cat and staff! How great this cat tree was! Completely new, wonderful rituals have developed as a result. From then on, when Flix came downstairs with me in the morning to make breakfast, he wanted to be rewarded first. With treats spread on his new cat tree, of course. So he completed his morning exercise straight away and rewarded himself with it. A classic win-win situation, I would say.

Over time, Flix found more and more occasions that were worthy of a reward, so he thought. Whenever he came into the kitchen, he wanted to be rewarded. I knew what to do; quickly get a few treats and spread them on the cat tree at different levels. Already cat and Cat Mum were happy. After the work was done, Flix usually rested from the exertion of earning his rewards.

Over time, Flix got bolder. He tried to get to the upper level of his new cat tree. First, he started to stretch himself so that he could grab treats on the first level. One day he managed to lift himself up onto the upper level. He looked around enthusiastically and sniffed everything. But he didn't want to stay. Quickly he got down again, first jumping elegantly to the middle and then all the way down.

One day, however, the experiment didn't go as planned. He jumped from the middle onto the upper level, but only made it to the edge. He sat with his back legs directly on the edge. Then he seemed to itch a little, he scratched himself, and crashed, fell backwards in a somersault.

Fortunately, he was a cat and not a dog. Even from this small height, he somehow managed to flip over and land on his legs. It hit me like an arrow through my heart, very difficult to describe. A big shock because a cat with vestibular syndrome should never fall on his head. Very big that nothing worse happened. For me and for him.

And that wasn't all. It happened again a short time later. Oh man. Of course he didn't let on about anything and ran away as fast as he could. I was concerned that his vestibular syndrome was getting worse, or it might be a seizure, and his balance was again out of order.

I then did a clearing first, with him and with me. That felt a lot better. Nevertheless, these events motivated me to make an appointment with the neurologist at the next kidney check-up so that he could have a look. Fortunately, I had a video of one of these falls.

HELLO MAX – CONVERSATIONS WITH DEPARTED ANIMALS

Now comes a chapter where you might shake your head and think: "Hmm, how is that supposed to work?" I can only say—it works. And, I had the privilege of learning it too. And yes, I also use it for my own and other animals. As with everything, the truth is that "Practice makes perfect."

As already described in the chapter "From an Energetic Viewpoint," everything is energy and everything is connected to everything else. Max's soul has moved on. He just left his body behind.

In my third seminar on animal communication in May, we covered the topics of communication with departed animals and communication with missing animals. The principle is the same. First you bring yourself into a relaxed state, bring the brain waves into a calm state, make contact through the eyes of the animal, and establish a heart connection. In my group doing the exercise, three people spoke to Max, and Sylvia did as well. What we all received from Max has given a well-rounded picture.

Max has a job in Rainbowland. He takes care of the newcomers. He said that there are many arrivals that never had it nearly as good as he did. His time with us was the best of his life, even when he was sick. Because he received so much love. He found it wonderful that he could leave in his own way. He said his soul had loosened like a rubber band and then he just flew away. That was exactly the feeling he had imagined and wished for. Just fly away when the time comes. He was happy where he was now. I was deeply touched. My heart was overflowing with love for my Max. And my eyes were full of tears.

He said that he would continue to accompany us because the task was not yet completed. And, he would send someone to us when it was the right timing.

I also met two great women in this third course, Kristin and Kerstin. Since then, we have always helped each other with our animals and with animals of clients. We have also supported each other on our individual paths.

I also had some wonderful conversations with Max. In many situations when animals were getting ready to go to Rainbowland, Max was always there. It became his job to take care of the newcomers, especially animals that Kristen and I worked with. Max was often there when the animal souls crossed the Rainbow Bridge.

The following is a particularly good conversation that shows Max's wisdom and the role he took with me. In 2019, I found a senior red cat on the Instagram account of the Mainz Animal Shelter. He moved me very much. And I seriously considered adopting him. Max saw it like this:

Max thinks I am reacting to the pattern "red cat" and I should get rid of it first.

In addition, the current timing would not be good because of the newly achieved level of harmony with Flix and Howy (Howy came to us in mid-2017. You will find out how in the next chapters) and also because of Howy's aches and pains—he doesn't think they're easy to handle ... he said ... *"stay tuned, absolutely!"*

"You can't do everything at the same time," he said ... he also reminded me of the soul cats book ... very seriously ... otherwise he is very satisfied with me, will continue to accompany me on my path ... I should learn to accept and implement everything that I experience, bit by bit. My teacher (Toby) would think highly of me. If he was demanding, it would be because he wanted to draw something out of me.

I told Max something else. My dear friend Fiona Oakes in England[1] lost Teddy Freddy today, a very old horse that already had

---

1. Tower Hill Stables Animal Sanctuary, Essex, UK, founded and run by Fiona Oakes. She cares for more than 500 rescued animals, cows, pigs, horses, sheep, chickens, turkeys, cats and dogs.

two strokes. When his horse friend William left a few weeks ago, it quickly became clear that Teddy Freddy would soon follow him.

"Can you check on Teddy Freddy, please?"

"Sure, it's my job here," he said proudly.

I thank you from the bottom of my heart, my dear Max!

———————

Great, Max knows and will see Teddy Freddy.
And that's how he did it.

THE UNIVERSE ARRANGED
EVERYTHING PERFECTLY

On July 19th, we had a check-up at the veterinary clinic because of Flix's blood pressure and his kidney test levels. To be precise, we had moved the date from July 21st to July 19th because I really wanted to have a neurology appointment for Flix. You remember that Flix's falls worried me, and I really wanted to have this checked neurologically. I had the sneaking feeling that the same polyp drama was going to play out in his other ear.

We both went with him to the appointment in the morning. Flix was energetically prepared and informed via animal communication that today was about his blood pressure and blood test, and the neurology appointment.

We came into the cat waiting room and sat down with Flix, and then a cat meowed. Heart-breaking. Like an arrow through the heart. And meowed again, actually incessantly. The humans of the meowing cat were from the Hanau Animal Shelter. The tomcat probably had some issues with the intestines and pancreas. He just kept meowing. I got into a conversation with the lady and we exchanged email addresses. I assured her that I would send her a document on alternative therapies for pancreatic disease. Then it was our turn. But the meowing never got out of my head and certainly not out of my heart. Howy was the name of the meowing cat ...

Flix's blood pressure was good, considering the circumstances. It was measured three times to get the correct number. You measure blood pressure until it stops falling; in this case it took three measurements, in other cases it can require more. Our vet, herself a cardiologist, attached great importance to ensuring that it was done correctly. Otherwise, cats will be given medication that they do not need. Flix's blood pressure was well regulated, his medication was kept at the same dose. Little Flix usually made himself comfortable on her lap for these procedures. Humming, of course. Then we moved to another cat consulting room and waited for the neurologist. As always with such appointments, I sent videos in advance so the vet had a chance to see what I had described.

After reviewing the videos and doing a general neurological examination, the neurologist was satisfied with our Flix. Yes, he thought that one fall indicated a seizure event. Nevertheless, he would not recommend any further diagnoses, especially if it did not occur frequently, since his general condition was good and he had mastered the situation very well for his 17 years.

Then we left the consulting room and passed by Howy and his humans again. Howy continued to meow ... hit me right in the heart ... every time.

We drove home with Flix; he let himself be pampered and indulged in a well-deserved rest.

I couldn't get Howy out of my head. My research on the website of the Hanau Animal Shelter revealed wonderful pictures of a small, gentle tomcat, 16 years old, who ended up in the animal shelter because of the death of his human caretaker. He had been there for a few months. Alone, grieving. He wanted a family so badly.

Howy ... it's him. He is the one Max wanted to send us when the time came. A gentle soul, a soul that wouldn't take advantage of Flix's situation. That was his requirement for a feline buddy. All these thoughts shot through my head.

I called the lady at the animal shelter, and she was very happy that I not only wanted to help her with Howy, but that we were actually interested in adopting him. We quickly made an appointment for the following Saturday so that we could get to know him—and of course he could get to know us too. I immediately obtained her consent that we could "talk" to Howy before our visit on Saturday.

OK, who else had to be asked? Max and Flix, of course:

I got in touch with Max. He was suddenly there, very present when I was lying on the sofa.

After some general banter, I asked him if he had sent us Howy. Yes! Howy desperately needs a family, he said. A wounded soul, with a few physical ailments. He needs love, care and a home where he is understood and accepted. He would be just the right friend for Flix, Max said. Howy was wise, gentle, by no means an alpha cat like himself. He would just let Flix be Flix. So everything is just right.

What would Flix say about that?

I explained everything to him, who Howy was, what kind of soul he was and what kind of problems he would bring with him. And, that he was Flix's age. Flix was pretty positive about the prospect. He said if Howy were really like I said, it should work out fine.

And Flix also said: *"If someone needs help, then we help!"*

Thank you, my dear Flix!

It was now time to get in touch with Howy as well. How nice that Kristin helped me so graciously. She also got in touch with him and Flix. Howy is very happy that we would come. He wished so much that he could meet loving humans and just be himself.

Kristin got this from Howy:

Yes, he would like to join us!!! But the feeling came immediately … This is perfect for Flix! Such a wonderful, gentle, and straight-forward tomcat; the way he looks at you reminds me of my Paulino! He's sad, he says, and he was pleasantly surprised to get a new buddy! He is so grateful! He really is a good fit for you! Take him to you!

The following Saturday, we visited Howy in Hanau. We spent an hour with him in his cat dwelling. He was very open and was happy that we visited him. After a few minutes, I was able to caress him in his cat cave. He was very excited and certainly wanted to do his best.

He came out of his cave and was unmistakably proud that he had visitors. He immediately snuggled up to Michael and then sat down in the center of his cat dwelling—and put down a little pile that actually belonged in the litter box. It was quite funny!

Howy moved in with us the following Monday!

HOWY MOVES IN WITH US

Howy is Max's legacy. No doubt about it. Max had already said in animal communications in May that he would continue to accompany us because his task was not yet finished. And the task was, I realized, to deepen my basic trust so that I would move ahead on my path. To find and live my mission.

I have known for a while that lack of trust is one of my core issues because of my energy clearing work. It was obvious that my life with Max and his legacy, Howy, played a major role in it.

That's why he gave me a tricky task that could only be completed with exactly this: trust. My task was to integrate Howy and put his health back on a stable footing, so that he could spend a few more beautiful years with us. In the first six weeks, my trust was put to the test.

Max being Max, he supported me wonderfully on this path. The first week of Howy's integration wasn't easy. For one thing, he was very nervous, which was normal. He came from the shelter to a new home that he first had to learn to trust. Then there was Flix, who had a high need for security and is our beloved "worrywart." He tends to think a lot and analyze in detail. We had to give Flix security and even more time so that his role was not endangered.

As a consequence, I had decided to keep Howy and Flix separated for the first few days. Very experienced "cat integrators" advised me to do this.

Kristin helped me from a distance, with her intuition and experience of a household with nine cats. And Ellen, who had seven cats at the time, also helped me greatly with Howy's integration. Cats are attached to their territory. If a new cat enters the territory and is allowed to go to any place at once, the resident cat feels threatened, or at least unsettled. It wouldn't be any different for us. Imagine a stranger walking in the door, sitting down in the living room, and announcing that he or she would now also be living here.

So I took Howy into Michael's office first. There he had his food, water, and a litter box. There was enough space, as well as climbing opportunities. Howy's nervousness was always expressed by meowing; constant meowing in a decisive tone, which always reminded me a little of a bleating sheep. Through this idiosyncrasy, we had already come to know and love him.

Then I brought the two together for an hour, always giving both treats at the same time. They learned to eat treats together, keeping less and less of a distance between them.

During this time, Flix changed his location habits. Since Howy's move-in, Flix had focused on the bedroom. He was either on the bed, under the bed, or on the side where he had both a blanket and a basket.

But, he often came downstairs to control things! He couldn't allow himself to miss anything. So Flix started walking up and down more and more often. Some days, he must have walked the circuit twenty times. His curiosity was too great and communicating *his* rules was certainly too important. He made it clear that he was the boss here. Over time, Howy dared to go to many different places and developed his preferences. In addition, the big cat tree belonged to him anyway, as Flix could no longer jump up on it due to his handicap.

Even if it didn't appear that way, the cat communication seemed to be working fine. Howy seemed to know that he wasn't allowed in the bedroom. He rarely came upstairs, only every few days in the evening, when he looked around the bathroom and bedroom and left after a few moments. Flix would be sitting in a tense state under the bed. If Howy was there a little too long, he was reminded with just one hiss from Flix that he actually had no business here. So he left and trotted back down the stairs.

On the other hand, Howy had conquered the sofa downstairs. My idea in the beginning was that we would be able to divide up seats on the sofa. Howy could sit on the outside while Flix would sit where he always sat. Unfortunately, nothing came of that. Flix didn't jump on the sofa anymore.

He would patrol past it every now and then, not without hissing to show that he was the boss here and was generously allowing the staff and Howy to use the sofa. Then he went back to the bedroom, his command center.

Flix tried to keep Howy at bay in everything he did. That was clear to see. He knew about his physical limitations due to the vestibular syndrome, which made him see everything wrong. One blow would be enough and he would lose his balance and endanger his position. It was imperative to avoid that. In addition, he could not take part in battles for certain places for the same reasons. So he needed a different strategy.

That's why Flix developed sounds that we didn't even know he was capable of making. Several hissing and grumbling sounds that didn't sound dangerous, like a real hiss, but helped him get his point across. The strategy was clear: on the one hand, he wanted to give Howy his space, but on the other, to show him his limits and make it unmistakably clear who the Boss Cat was here.

Howy, conversely, longed for more contact and interaction with his new friend. He tried to get in physical contact with Flix. In the beginning, he was not always skillful. Howy loved to participate with his front paws on many occasions. He also approached Flix in the same way. "Hey buddy," the right paw seemed to say as it landed somewhere on Flix, mostly in the head area. Not so good because Flix immediately fell over. Then he snapped at Howy and purposefully went his way as quickly and firmly as he could.

Further practice grabbing treats together was on the schedule. That seemed to work out better and better. It also happened more often that Howy sniffed Flix's butt and vice versa. Flix usually did this when Howy was in the litter box, with its back facing the entrance. That's how he felt safe.

August and September brought many sunny days, when Flix spent entire mornings on the loggia in the sun. Howy seemed to know this was Flix's territory, too. But he came out with me for lunch on the front balcony or joined me for dinner. Flix did that far less frequently. So they balanced each other out.

The farther we got into the fall season, the more Flix made himself comfortable in the bedroom.

HOWY NEEDS TO GO TO THE CLINIC

Howy came with baggage: mental, emotional, and physical. The reason why he was at the veterinary clinic, where we first met him, was a rather complex problem consisting of chronic pancreatitis, recurrent biliary congestion, liver cysts, and mild diarrhea. We were given an extensive medication regimen. He was supposed to take his cortisone for another two weeks, and soaked psyllium husks were to be mixed in with his food to stop his diarrhea.

At the same time, he had to get used to his new home, which was stressful. Everything went well for the first few days and he ate well. However, after two weeks his appetite decreased when we were asked to taper off the cortisone. Unfortunately, he was not reacting well to it. He ate less and less and his gaze spoke volumes. "No, I am not feeling well, I am really sick." When all medication, naturopathic as well as pharmaceutical, failed to improve his condition, I took him to the veterinary clinic in Hofheim.

He had only been with us for a few weeks; it now was September. And, I was at the end of my game. Howy was not doing well at all. When we got to the emergency service at an advanced hour, it quickly became clear that Howy had to be admitted to the clinic. Oh dear, I didn't like that at all. What would he think? But there was nothing else I could do. Howy's life was on the line, so he should be given the best possible support. So I went home without him.

Howy stayed at the clinic for the weekend. He was given IV fluids and was put on new medication. Whenever I got a call from the veterinary clinic, I heard Howy in the background. He made himself heard. The ward doctor said that he kept everyone on their toes, and that they either talked to him or had to clean his box. So, he had everyone under control there too. And everyone loved him.

I picked him up the next Monday. Our Howy finally came home and his life with his new family could now continue. I was given an extensive medication regimen: cortisone, gastric acid inhibitors, something against the congestion of the bile system, and also psyllium husks for his diarrhea. Everything was explained to me; I should please bring him back for a check-up in ten days to see whether the therapy was working well, and whether anything else needed to be changed.

Howy was happy to get home and was doing a lot better, too. He was happy again, commented a lot and had a good appetite. We could take a deep breath for now.

The check-up appointment outcome was positive, his ultrasound showed him much more relaxed than two weeks earlier. It was clear, however, that his pancreas was permanently damaged and we had to keep an eye on his cystic liver lesions.

The vet was pleasantly surprised at how well he had recovered despite his advanced age. She explained to me that Howy would have to be on cortisone for the rest of his life, albeit on a lower dose. It was the only way to keep his complex symptoms under control. When I asked about the side effects of a long-term cortisone regimen, the vet said that cats would show few side effects, and that Howy would probably no longer experience them due to his old age.

I wasn't particularly happy with that. But I also realized that the prior efforts to get off the cortisone, after consulting the vet, had become quite dangerous for Howy. I wouldn't take any more chances in that regard. If he needed it, if it gave him a good quality of life, then he should get cortisone. This was about his life, not mine. About his quality of life. And certainly not about one ideology or another.

Howy seemed to agree wholeheartedly with the vet. In the office, he strutted across her desk and keyboard, went into his transport carrier by himself and looked at me. "Can we now please go back home?" Yes, that's exactly what we're doing.

NIGHTLY CAT SCREAMS AND OTHER CHALLENGES

If you've experienced this before, you know what I'm talking about! The screams of our cats are quite harrowing experiences. So loud it makes you sit upright in bed. Or, it prevents you falling asleep in the first place. We experienced all variations with Howy and later also with Flix.

The causes and backgrounds why older cats in particular scream at night have not really been determined. From my experience, there are various reasons. But one thing at a time.

Max had never screamed at night. In Max's times, Flix never screamed at night either. The first experience we had with nocturnal cat screams was with Howy.

When Howy came to us he was, as already mentioned, very stressed physically, emotionally, and mentally. One stress was related to the other. His trauma, how he got to the shelter, had to do with the fact that he had lost his human caretaker, and it probably took some time for that to be discovered. Apparently, he was brought to the shelter by the fire brigade. He kept showing this picture in animal communication, of how he was picked up by a person wearing gloves and taken to the shelter together with his partner cat, with whom he did not have a good relationship. Howy was probably just tagging along, but the other cat was the focus. Everything had hurt him very much and also traumatized him.

Then he no longer had a home. His stress and emotional injuries were mirrored in various physical symptoms from the pancreas to the intestine.

He came into his new home with us, and he needed to settle into the place. Reduce stress. Breathe. Get to know everything. At first he couldn't believe how many cat beds, blankets, and cat trees now belonged to him. He ran excitedly from one to the other, not knowing for a long time what his favorite spot would be. There were so many options.

As is so often the case when external circumstances calm down and relaxation occurs, body and soul realize that all other problems can now be tackled.

That explains why during the first few weeks in his new home, his various inflammations in the pancreas and intestines flared up again, and he both peed and screamed at night. I have already told you about the weekend stay at the clinic. Now let's talk about the screaming and peeing.

He used one of his beds every night to empty his bladder. It wasn't a classic pee in the sense of marking. No, he simply couldn't control and coordinate everything at the same time, because he had to deal with so many new things. He also told me that during our animal communication. How wonderful that we had this opportunity to better understand what was going on with our beloved Howy. It wasn't a problem during the day; he always went to his litter box.

I washed his bed every day for the first few weeks. Now that I knew what caused it, I also worked with him energetically. He got an aura clearing and a karma clearing. Kristin had also worked a lot with him in this regard. Lo and behold: We listened to him and things got better. After a few weeks, we had the nocturnal pee problem under control.

Howy was very communicative. The nocturnal screaming, however, came later. At that point, Howy was spending most of the night in one of his favorite spots in the living room. His screaming either started as soon as we were about to go to bed, or it started very early in the morning.

Well, at 16 years of age, Howy was an elderly tomcat, and the screaming started when he had gained nearly another year. The classic thesis is dementia. But Howy was not demented. I've been watching that closely. He was never disoriented, not even before his death. He also never wandered around screaming.

On the contrary, he screamed while sitting in his bed. So I proceeded to work energetically again. In the case of karmic blockages, the soul usually cannot process and dissolve everything at once. It's like with an onion. As soon as you have peeled off one layer, the next one comes to light. And so it was with Howy. We cleared the first rough blockages in the first six months. He stabilized mentally and physically.

Then it was apparently time for his soul to come up with the next layer of karmic issues. Howy's issues often had to do with a lack of self-esteem, limitations, dependencies, and relationship problems, specifically about "not being seen" or "not being listened to." That's probably the reason why he "told" us so much by screaming.

Yes, he was heard by us. We would listen. Always. He knew that his soul could heal here. So I cleared some of his karmic blockages, little by little. After a few months, we had the screaming mostly under control. How grateful I was again that I knew and could use these methods.

Flix didn't start screaming until much later. But with him it had a different reason. It was the Boss Cat's message to the family that everything was fine. He made his patrols very regularly. The one patrol early in the morning, around five o'clock, I remember, was apparently so important that we all had to be alerted to it immediately. And, it also had something to do with "letting the boss out" against Howy. But we'll talk about that in the chapter "Boss Cat Flix."

So Straight Into the Little Mouth

We had to accept the fact that Howy needed to take medication on a regular basis. Some of it was not a problem, as it was easy to pulverize and mix with the food. Other things—cortisone to be precise—were a little more difficult to administer. It apparently had an unpleasant smell, so the route via food did not work. So straight into the little mouth.

Over time, I developed a routine to ensure how the tablet could be put into his mouth and how it stayed there.

Initially, various YouTube videos provided great help in mastering the processes, at least theoretically. Unfortunately, the cats in the video are super loving and cooperative; they accept the individual steps without hesitation and just remain seated. Howy is quite cooperative, but he's also quite fidgety. That made it all a little difficult. Since he is a rather small, delicate tomcat, he sometimes slips through your fingers. And, you can find the tablet behind the sofa or under the table. Then I found a way: with empty capsules that taste like chicken. This became a routine that worked well. We used it until our cat sitter introduced the ingenious trick of squeezing the cortisone into a piece of sausage. This has since become the preferred method.

Howy stabilized, got better week after week, and even gained some weight. Thin as he was, weighing 5.7 lbs., he could use every little piece of food. So, we were on the upswing. Everything came together and Howy really caught on with us, with Flix, with living his new life.

I was happy that I learned how to administer the cortisone, especially since I could see how his condition stabilized and how he got better every day. Still, I wanted to give him something that not only suppressed symptoms but also helped support his stressed pancreas.

After previous positive experience with medicinal mushrooms, I made up my mind to add Coprinus[1]. As always, we started sneaking it in, giving only small amounts of the medicinal mushroom. When Howy had accepted it well, I slowly increased the dosage and he was given half a capsule of the mushroom powder throughout the day. And, it was good for him. He continued to regenerate and also gained additional weight. His fur began to shine again and he became a vital, happy, senior dream cat.

---

1. Coprinus comatus (shaggy ink cup): In veterinary medicine Coprinus is mainly used for sarcomas and pancreatic diseases. It regenerates the pancreas in pancreatitis and promotes digestion. Source: https://mykotroph.de/en/animals-coprinus-comatus-en/

FLIX'S DENTAL RESTORATION

Flix's dental restoration had actually been planned for much earlier, but the vestibular syndrome and long recovery prevented that. And then Howy came to us.

The original date planned in September therefore no longer made sense. Flix had told Kristin that he didn't want the procedure at this point because the newly established harmony with Howy would be disturbed. What a wise cat, my little Flix! At first, he didn't want the dental restoration at all, and then he said maybe next summer. I put the topic to rest for now.

With feline seniors, it is important to carefully weigh what should be done taking a long-term perspective before a real problem arises, which then requires immediate action, even if it is anything but good timing. Flix was in the first stage of CKD and, based on the estimates of the animal shelter, he was older than Max. It was important to keep an eye on the vestibular syndrome and the CKD and to help him get stronger, giving him the best possible support. That also included tackling any issues with foresight, as long as he was doing well. And the teeth were definitely an issue, especially with CKD, as we had learned from Max.

A few weeks later, I discussed it with him again. We agreed on late November. He accepted my arguments but didn't really want to do it. But, he understood why it was important to me and why it was also the recommendation of his vet.

A few days before the appointment, I felt a scratch with some scab behind his right ear. Where did that come from? We knew that he often shook himself and scratched his ear. He's been prone to it since his ear surgery. But, he had never developed ear mites or anything like that.

I took Flix to the clinic in the morning. He seemed to know exactly what was on the program and looked at me for a long time. "Well, if you think so," he seemed to be saying. I explained to him again on the drive that everything was only for his best. Of course, he wasn't enthusiastic about it.

At our vet's office, I showed her the scratches on his ear. They would look at it while he was anesthetized. He was immediately hooked up to an IV and was given another infusion because of his kidneys, before the dental restoration began an hour later. I should get a call from the dentist around 1 p.m.

I drove home again, did some work, always with the phone next to me. On days like this, it's difficult to get anything done in a reasonable way. But I've developed a certain routine of distracting myself with work. Soon it was 1 p.m. and I waited longingly for the call from the clinic. It didn't come. I became more and more nervous. At 2 p.m., the dentist called and told me that little Flix had taken a lot of time to wake up, but that he was now sitting up and holding his head up. Thank God!

She explained that his teeth had been professionally cleaned, that the dental X-rays were done, and that a tooth that had been obstructing another had been removed. Best of all was the all-clear: it was not FORL, which would have affected a whole row of teeth.

He continued to receive IV fluids and I picked him up later that afternoon. My vet handed him over to me and informed me about his ears. He had yeast of the genus Malassezia (a genus of fungi) in his ear. Something new again. In the right ear, exactly on the side where the open scratch marks were. He was to get ear drops and I should have his ears checked again in ten days, then by the dermatologist. She warned me right away that Flix had absolutely no desire to let anyone near his ears today. Great. Lots of fun ahead!

I drove home with Flix, where Howy had already missed him. He was visibly relieved that his buddy was back. Flix had undergone enough that day for now. Alright, we would tackle the ear drops tomorrow.

To cut a long story short: the plan for the ear drops did not work out. Flix vehemently refused to have them dripped in his ear. He got downright aggressive and escaped every attempt faster than I could even blink.

During the appointment with the dermatologist, I explained the situation and emphasized that we absolutely needed another therapy. Flix was given an oral anti-fungal drug, which would make the therapy a few weeks longer. I didn't care, as long as we had a way to solve the problem without ear drops.

At the same time, I educated myself about medicinal mushrooms and consulted directly with Mykotroph[1]. Lo and behold, there was a certain mix of mushrooms—Hericium/Shiitake—that had proven to be effective against Malassezia. I ordered the mix for him and we started sneaking it into his medicinal mushroom powder. He accepted that well.

We got rid of the Malassezia with no further problems within a couple of weeks. But we need to add Howy's part of the story …

1. Mykotroph is an Institute for natural health and vital mushrooms in Germany. Source: https://mykotroph.de/en/

Boss Cat Flix

Flix had spent the months following Max's death alone with us. It was easy to be the Boss Cat in this situation. Nobody contested his position. Nevertheless, we were able to observe a wonderful transformation during this time. Flix, who had relied on Max's judgment in everything, now had to make his own decisions.

Was the loggia safe enough to lie out in the sun? Which litter box should he use? Should he sleep downstairs or upstairs? And most importantly, how should he manage his staff? He was now responsible for that, too ...

He developed a whole new level of strength, great self-confidence, and much more trust in himself and his surroundings. He was rightly proud of himself for having learned so many new things. Every step he learned again, be it walking up the stairs, jumping on the sofa, or jumping on the little cat tree, increased his self-confidence. He really surpassed all expectations.

Well, with Howy's move-in, it was a little more complicated. Since Flix by nature is a gentle tomcat who runs away into his own territory rather than attacking an intruder, the selection of an equally gentle tomcat was very important. A cat that, unlike Max, was not an alpha animal. Since Max knew that Flix would "have some problems" in these areas, he sent us Howy.

As soon as Howy moved in, even when we kept them separated, Flix began to change his habits. Just as we expected, he first withdrew into his own territory. Into the bedroom which, from then on, became his residence.

When the two of them got along better and adjusted to each other, it became clear that it was important to Flix to demonstrate, from time to time, who's boss. He knew that he was less able to defend himself physically. So he made the most amazing hissing sounds to tell Howy that he was the boss here. And, like Max before, he took the liberty of stealing food from Howy.

Howy, on the other hand, was very wise. He accepted it when Flix called him to order and thought to himself, "Go ahead. I'm sitting down here on the sofa anyway!" Besides, Howy didn't want to be the boss at all, he just wanted to participate. The interaction was important to him. With us and with Flix. And he wanted to have fun, to experience joy.

When Howy had hunkered down in the middle of the red carpet in front of the kitchen and blocked the passage, Flix sat a few feet away with a sad face and waited until the path was clear. Often he waited a long time when Howy was enjoying lounging on the carpet. Howy would have loved to fool around with Flix. But Flix wouldn't allow him to do that. Flix ran past him, not without sounding an appropriate boss warning.

Even if Howy was sitting on the sofa and Flix patrolled past it, Howy could playfully give him a light blow; always with the right front paw, like a reflex. Flix dodged and ran past, not without commenting on the action in a disapproving manner. Sometimes, when Howy had to be called to order as far as Flix was concerned, Flix first sat up, then backed up and hit Howy with a paw. This was followed by a "boss-like" walk-off. Howy was mostly unimpressed, but he let Flix triumph. How wise of dear Howy.

Since Flix's ear surgery, I have always praised him repeatedly for everything he had to learn; knowing how important it was to him, I continued doing that. It was very motivating for him to be praised and recognized.

Ever since Howy's move-in, Flix had managed to win or defend his own way of being the Boss Cat. He said in late 2017 how proud he was about being the boss and that Howy respected and recognized him. Nobody has ever praised him *for that*. However, he didn't say it that clearly; instead he developed the yeast in the ears.

When the ears become sick, the question arises as to how much the patient feels he has not been heard. I examined all areas of our life and couldn't come up with a real cause. Much has changed since Howy arrived here. And, in October and November, I had one or two business trips that lasted more than two days. We had organized ourselves in such a way that

Michael worked from home or took a few days off, so that the two tomcats were looked after and cared for in the best possible way. For our highly sensitive Flix, who liked to over-analyze everything, it could have been too much coming and going that stressed him out. He wanted one thing above all as Boss Cat: to keep the family together. For him, that meant everyone was at home following their usual rhythm, and that routine prevailed, because changes were not his thing.

In January 2018, we had another crisis with Howy. He'd been off his eating pattern for a few days and didn't seem to be doing very well. On Saturday, he refused any food. It often happened that he didn't eat anything until noon, and only then began to eat his breakfast. On that day, however, he didn't eat any of the regular food, nor a second variety of food, nor a third or fourth one. He sniffed it and walked away again. He had also vomited white foam twice.

OK, I thought to myself, after giving him cortisone in the evening it will surely get better. Unfortunately, that was not the case. He vomited again, including the cortisone tablet. And he looked really miserable. He wasn't doing well at all. He felt nauseous, that was more than obvious.

We'd already had one or two crises with Howy and we knew how complex his issues were. I could tell he was doing badly. So, take no chances, pack up your cat and drive to the veterinary clinic.

Nobody chooses emergency service on a Saturday evening. There weren't many animals in the waiting area. But, those who were there all urgently needed a vet. Emergencies were then prioritized and it wasn't our turn until around two o'clock in the morning. Luckily, we weren't one of the emergencies that needed immediate attention because of an acute danger to life. In this respect, one gladly waits.

Then it was our turn; the vet had already looked at Howy's patient file, examined him, listened to him. He diagnosed an acute attack of pancreatitis. We both concluded that Howy would best recover at home. He would be injected with cortisone and vitamin B12, and we would go home again. Fortunately, this episode wasn't as bad as the one in September when he had to stay at the clinic.

As soon as Howy heard that he was allowed to come home with me, his face lit up immediately. Indeed, animals understand everything that is said. And they answer. Just not in our language. Even the vet was amazed when he noticed Howy's suddenly changed demeanor. With Howy now bolstered by vitamin B12 and a cortisone injection, we drove home again. Howy was visibly better. He was talking again.

We got home a little before three o'clock in the morning. Michael was still awake, and I hardly believed it when he told me that Flix had been sitting with him on the sofa most of the time. That was it! His job was to keep us all together! That was very important to him. Keeping control and worrying about Howy, which he always did when Howy was not doing well, was part of the job.

Flix feels responsible for all of us. He took that over from Max. That's a heavy burden. But, *that* was something I didn't hear: Flix needed a lot more praise and recognition in his Boss Cat role. This became expressed through the Malassezia in his ear.

Since that day, I started praising Flix to the skies for each of his Boss Cat activities. And Flix's change was obvious. His eyes became clear again. Very clear, bright and big. Then it was no problem getting rid of the yeast in his ears. Three weeks later, no more yeast was found in the ear swab.

CAT DAD'S HOWY OR WHO TAKES CARE OF WHAT

It was obvious: those two had found each other here! Howy had become very close to Michael. That became apparent early on, actually at the shelter when we visited Howy. As soon as Michael sat on the floor with him, Howy snuggled up very close.

When Howy came to us, he had to learn that his Cat Dad was not there four days a week, but usually came home on Thursday evening. It was all the more satisfying to see how happy Howy was when his "buddy" came home.

Howy developed into a "coach potato," enjoyed sitting down with his Cat Dad on the sofa in the evenings, preferably cuddling on his right side in the crook of his arm. It became a fixed ritual for both of them!

Howy closely monitored Michael's working hours. If he couldn't seem to finish in the evening, or if he worked too long from Howy's point of view, there were clear messages. Howy went into Michael's study and announced loudly that the working day was over. It was like he picked his Cat Dad up from work.

Later, in the final months of his life when he slept a lot in bed with us, Howy snuggled in the crook of Michael's arm. Many Sunday afternoons were also celebrated in this way. It was just lovely to see how this petite, noisy tomcat, well under 6.5 lbs., declared his 6 feet 4 inches tall Cat Dad to be his favorite person.

Howy has clearly shown us which tasks each of his favorite people should perform. He gave us clear roles. Whenever he was not feeling well, if his pancreas or gallbladder was causing him pain again and we had to go to the vet or animal health practitioner, or if he needed medication, he turned to me. He expressed this in various animal communications: when it came to visits to the vet, therapy, medication, I was his first choice. He accepted all the decisions that we made together for him. He accepted it when I had to decide something quickly.

Over time, I became very experienced in administering tablets when he needed them. Even when it came to dispensing something into the mouth. Practice makes perfect. Over time, I became skillful and, above all, confident in handling syringes, pill dispensers, and capsules.

Whenever I asked Michael to do medicines for me, it was usually unsuccessful. Simply because Cat Dad was too apprehensive, so that Howy immediately sensed this insecurity and left deftly—without medication, of course.

This is also an example that loving but consistent action gives animals security. They understand whether or not they need certain medications. Whenever one of the cats had steadfastly refused to take a certain drug, such as Flix with his gastrointestinal problem, then there was an underlying reason for it. From my point of view, it is important to respect that. The drug is then literally not on the "same wavelength," which means not on the same energy frequency as the animal.

HOWY'S POST-CORTISONE-PERIOD

Summer 2018 was approaching. Howy was doing well and we had learned to deal with any minor crises and relapses ourselves. For some time now, we had stopped administering the acid blocker, and then also stopped the drug that regulated the biliary stasis, since he no longer showed any signs of biliary colic. Everything was done in coordination with his vet at the clinic. What remained was the cortisone therapy and his medicinal mushrooms.

After Howy's blood test, the vet raised the issue of continuing cortisone for the first time. I should lower the dosage; apparently he didn't need it anymore, at least not in this dosage. OK, will do. But how should we sneak it out? Give half the amount every other day and then reduce it little by little to the lower dose.

It didn't work that way. Howy seemed more stressed than before; unfortunately changing the quantities did not mean that we could settle on the lower dose. There were always bad days, and due to my not knowing any better, I gave him the higher dosage again.

Howy was now sending clear signals that he no longer wanted cortisone. He accepted the pills with increasing reluctance. We needed to find other ways. It was all too much for him. He developed dizziness and a headache, according to my friend Kristin who helped us tremendously at this time. She obtained this information through doing a body scan of Howy during her animal communication.

At the next blood test, we were facing an inevitable result of cortisone therapy, although my vet had tried to spare me this development: the fructosamine level had increased. We faced an acute danger that Howy would develop diabetes. It was important to avoid that at all costs. Now we had to get away from cortisone. Absolutely.

My vet's message was clear. It's serious! I explained to her that we needed a different course of action to taper it off to suit Howy. I was then given smaller 1 mg cortisone tablets and a plan to lower the cortisone by 0.5 mg every ten days. We fared much better with that. I spoke to Howy and explained to him that we could get off cortisone. That we would now reduce the dosage little by little. He understood all of this. Since Howy was doing well with this process, we were even able to accomplish weekly reductions in dosage.

Why do you have to taper off cortisone anyway, you might ask yourself? Good question. The body normally produces cortisol in the adrenal cortex. If this substance is supplied from the outside, the body's own production stops over time. If the cortisone from the outside were to be abruptly discontinued, the body would soon go into shock because it cannot restart its own production so quickly. Then there is a risk of adrenal insufficiency. Therefore, you have to taper cortisone therapy off slowly so that the body has enough time to ramp up its own cortisol production again.

At the same time, I was looking for alternatives. How could I support Howy in the long run and keep his shaky pancreas and cystic liver and general health at a good level?

I, or rather Kristin, found an animal health practitioner in our town: bioresonance[1] and traditional Chinese medicine (TCM) were his specialties. I called and left a message. I received a call back late that evening. Yes, of course we could come see him. However, he could not promise anything, these are intricate relationships. But he would do his best to help Howy so that he could be stabilized without cortisone in the long run.

---

1. Bioresonance is a form of holistic diagnosis and therapy. It is claimed that the bioresonance devices used in the therapy can read the energy wavelengths coming from cells within the body and that the frequencies of these wavelengths provide information about the health of the body. Practitioners believe they can interpret the results obtained from the devices which can then be used to diagnose diseases or adverse medical conditions. Some practitioners also claim to use the results to treat the diagnosed conditions by using the same electromagnetic frequencies to create a "resonance" within the body's cells.
Source: https://www.asa.org.uk/advice-online/bioresonance-therapy.html

A few days later, we had our first appointment. The practice dog Faust immediately took a liking to Howy. As it turned out, Faust loved cats and he and Howy became very good friends.

Howy was examined using the TCM method and placed on a bioresonance mat. He could stay in his cat carrier for all of this, I just took off the lid. He observed and participated in everything with great interest, and immediately commented loudly in his usual way. Howy's meowing endeared him immediately to everyone there. As I said before, his meowing sounds more like sounds of a sheep. But that's exactly what makes Howy so unique.

The treatment was visibly good for him. He received the bioresonance program imprinted on globules. Bioresonance works energetically, first making a scan to identify areas that are out of energetic balance, then initiating programs to restore the balance again. Medications that energetically fit the patient's issues are used, their frequencies imprinted on globules. These globules are taken home and administered daily. We should come back in two weeks and continue tapering off the cortisone during that time.

I had a very good feeling. Howy did too. He was looking forward to everything new that was already underway. He had enough of taking pills. He communicated this with every fiber of his being.

He received his bioresonance globules twice a day in a small amount of cat cream, which he gratefully accepted. And, he kept taking his medicinal mushrooms. He no longer needed psyllium husks because his digestion was stable.

Contrary to the warnings of the animal health practitioner, Howy mastered tapering off of the cortisone without a crisis, without further pancreatitis flare-up. All good.

Except for the fact that he lost weight again. Due to the cortisone, he had gained weight up to 7.7 lbs. Now he lost weight steadily. He was already a rather slim, petite, but long-legged type of cat.

I was so happy that we had found a good way to continue supporting Howy in our post-cortisone period. I admit that the trigger of the increased fructosamine level caused me to work hard to stabilize him without cortisone. Anyone who has treated animals with chronic diseases using cortisone will agree with me that it is, at first, a "convenient" method because the cortisone initially covers up symptoms. The animal is doing better, apparently fine. I say apparently because we know that this will not treat the causes of disease, but will calm the whole system so that the symptoms abate. And yes, our little tigers usually get better at first. With cat like Howy who has little appetite, you are happy when he puts on a little weight.

Then, as caretaker you are relieved that a way has been found that provides the animal a good quality of life. There's nothing wrong with that. The problem arises precisely when the management of the acute flare-up of a chronic illness becomes the permanent treatment. That was exactly what we were facing with Howy. How and when can you get off this?

One must not forget that cortisone is already upsetting the hormonal balance in the body. A new equilibrium must be established as cortisone is withdrawn. That takes months and requires support. If this phase is not supported and there is a relapse or other complication, then unfortunately you often hear: "You won't be able to manage it anymore without cortisone." This is usually not the case. Most of the time, the body was not given enough time and support to "start up again." Our animal health practitioner told us from the beginning that this phase can be bumpy.

What most animals lack in their treatment is a holistic approach that brings their entire system back into balance while the cortisone is slowly tapered off. I am very grateful that we were able to make this possible for Howy with bioresonance and TCM.

When we checked his blood again a few weeks later, we were all—Howy, me, our vet and our animal health practitioner—very relieved. The fructosamine level was back in the normal range! We had just avoided diabetes in the nick of time. I was especially happy for Howy; he really had enough ailments to deal with.

Our dear friend Wally had an even older female cat that had been diabetic since she was 11 years old and was cared for in an exemplary manner. So we would have had the very best training. Still, it's better not to let the problem arise in the first place.

MEDICAL COMEBACK-CAT

It was late August 2018. We had just settled in without cortisone. We mastered the whole process of tapering it off without a crisis, much to the astonishment of our animal health practitioner Tom.

The flare-up came quite suddenly. Howy felt sick, it was difficult for him to eat; he went to the food, walked away, came back again, and walked away again from sheer nausea. Tom did acupuncture on him, advising that if he didn't eat later today, he would have to go to the vet tomorrow and probably needed an infusion.

After acupuncture, he felt better and took a few bites. Unfortunately, it wasn't enough and the next morning he was quite nauseous again. He could not eat or drink. He started to get dehydrated. So, I grabbed him and off we went to the veterinary clinic.

Howy was examined thoroughly, the blood test levels did not show any significant changes compared to the previous results a few weeks earlier. The ultrasound did not reveal any findings that we did not already know.

Without cortisone, Howy had become as skinny again as when he had come to us. The weight we really wanted him to maintain was 5.9 lbs. It didn't always work. Each flare-up caused him to lose weight. We were often at only 5.5 lbs., his current weight. The internist who took care of him said: "You do know that Howy is a very, very old cat." Of course I knew that. But look at him, note how much will to live he exudes. That convinced them. Not just once has he been described as a medical miracle, but also as a medical "comeback cat."

The older he got, the harder it became for him to regain weight. Even if he ate well from the healthiest and finest foods, including fresh chicken, gaining a few ounces was nearly impossible.

In this situation, he was given an IV infusion and feeding. We went back to the waiting area with the IV pole, where I could do some work. Howy entertained the audience there; a cancer-stricken dog was there with her Dog Dad for therapy. And Howy, who was sick himself, encouraged her. I was immensely proud of my Howy!

After two hours, he started eating again. This took a huge load off my heart. Immediately, he was back in his element, radiating joy and optimism, commenting on the event. "Let's go home."

Sure, we'll do that! We just have to pay the bill quickly. As always, he commented on that as well, much to the amusement of the ladies at the veterinary clinic's reception desk. No question, he was feeling much better, he was the same old Howy again!

MOMENTS ON THE BALCONY

Howy became a real balcony and loggia cat over time. Because he wanted to take part in everything, he developed different ways of actively participating in our meals. From spring to late summer, whenever we were either on the loggia or on the balcony, Howy was there.

He joined me for breakfast on weekdays, when I was mostly alone. He came out with me, jumped on the garden table, and took a seat right in front of my breakfast. Just like Max, he loved spending those morning moments with me. At the same time, he let the morning sun shine on his fur.

Whenever I, or Michael and I, had the pleasure of enjoying breakfast with Howy on the loggia, the day couldn't start off any better. It was such a wonderful, deep connection that we all treasured. To see Howy enjoying his life, lounging in the sun, was just wonderful. Max had exactly the same breakfast habits in the summer. He had been happy to be there with us, also choosing to lie on the garden table and enjoy the morning sun.

When Howy experienced crises, which happened quite often, I offered him his various food options outside. I always put food where he just happened to be. He mostly accepted it gratefully. It often happened that he dined with me, or with us. And there was a reason for it. Howy was easily distracted. As soon as he heard or saw something, he looked up. Usually everything else was more interesting than his food. If one of us wasn't there, he just ran away from the food. He liked to dine with company. Even if he was distracted by us and constantly looked up, his humans were right next to him and he mostly stayed with his food. Howy was a definite snack eater, a nibble here, a nibble there. Just a feline habit.

At lunchtime, I was usually on the balcony eating lunch or drinking coffee. And of course, Howy joined me. He loved being outside, participating and keeping me company. Most of the time, he wanted to jump on my lap and then run across the table. When I was alone, he liked to sit in the garden chair across from me. Very cute. We experienced many unforgettable moments like this.

FLIX'S KIDNEY CRISIS, TAKE 1

It was late summer 2018. After Howy had improved so much with his new care from our animal health practitioner, Tom, I wanted to give Flix this treatment as well. I asked Tom to take a look at him from a TCM point of view and see what bioresonance had to say. Of course, I was very interested in how we could support Flix's CKD, which had been stable to date.

So, I set up a double appointment for both Howy and Flix. Packed up both cats and drove to the other end of town. Usually, Flix could easily be put in his transport carrier. But, that day he growled when I put him in. He was otherwise in good shape, a good eater; defecation and peeing were working all right. His fur, however, had become somewhat "kidney-pelted." Cats with CKD often have fur in the kidney area that is oily, less shiny, and with scale. All the more important for him to be treated today.

Since Howy, barely contained in the cat carrier, commented on the situation almost non-stop, he was looked at first. I'll never do that again. Keeping the Boss Cat waiting is not a good idea. For many reasons. One is that it undermines his status. Another was a pressing problem that only arose in this situation.

After Howy was treated, it was Flix's turn. I opened his box, took him out and was startled. He exuded a strong urine-like odor. That was not the case at home. Definitely not. He had never smelled like this at all. What had happened in the past hour? I told Tom in a nutshell what

Flix's health issues were: CKD, vestibular syndrome, and head tilted slightly since then.

Tom was shocked because Flix had this strong urine-like odor, and immediately went into crisis assessment mode. Me too. What happened in less than an hour? Tom felt all organs, took his pulse TCM-style. Flix growled incessantly, as he always did when he was stressed. He was placed on the bioresonance mat and specifically tested for the kidneys and bladder. Everything pointed to an acute retention of urine, which would back up into the kidney if not remedied as quickly as possible.

Tom suggested giving him an acupuncture treatment immediately. Flix wasn't familiar with that yet. I picked him up and he allowed all the needles to be inserted, albeit he wasn't very enthusiastic about it. But, somehow he felt that he was being helped. After a few minutes, he relaxed. I was given instructions on what to look out for at home.

Shortly after we arrived at home, Flix was finally able to urinate. And he did a lot. So glad! I was completely exhausted. How could such a situation develop in just a few hours? I had learned something again.

Tom explained it to me like this: It was obvious that he had grain-like urinary stones, very small, called renal gravel. This had not previously been noticed in urine tests done from urine we had brought to the clinic. And, we hadn't had an ultrasound exam done in a long time. However, if the little grains changed so much that urinary retention arose, it could unfortunately become very dangerous within a few hours. That was exactly what we were facing.

What a blessing in disguise that we were in the right place at the right time, and that he could be helped immediately. Once again, a nice example that the universe orchestrates very skillfully exactly what is needed; something we then call "blessing in disguise." As I had learned in many other situations, it was divine right timing.

MOTHER-IN-LAW ON DUTY

Flix and Howy knew my mother-in-law Anneliese from several visits, so it was quite natural for them to accept her as temporary "staff." They both loved her from the bottom of their hearts, and Anneliese knew quite well how to handle them. Even in Max's time, she often stayed with us and had a great relationship with all the cats.

The two cats were well looked after at home when once in a while we both were traveling together. We took trips to England in 2018 and Mecklenburg-Western Pomerania in 2019, and Anneliese was there; she lived with us and did a tremendous job looking after both of them.

What we know from Anneliese's stories is that the two always arranged their time with her perfectly. That was great for Howy, because Anneliese had a lot more time for him and could cuddle with him on the sofa for several hours a day. Heavenly situation for Howy! From time to time, he tried to "help" knit socks, I was told. As always, he had a lot of fun "participating" with his front paws.

Anneliese also helped us out when Max was with us. One of the most moving moments for her was when Max said goodbye. It was early December 2016, when we already knew that he had metastasis in his lymph node. She was staying with us for a few days for Michael's birthday. On the last day, Max came to her bed in the morning and said goodbye. She often said later that, at that moment, she knew clearly Max wanted to say goodbye. It was the way he had looked at her. His eyes could be very penetrating. You could read a lot in them. Anneliese has a keen sense for this and was very moved by that particular moment.

Max knew exactly what to expect. And he designed his departure very consciously.

Vitamin B12

In early 2019, our Howy was still suffering from vomiting. I brought it up at his next routine check-up, and his vitamin B12 level was tested. It was so low that it could no longer be measured.

You may wonder how that can happen with a carnivore. That's exactly what I asked myself! Michael and I supplement with vitamin B12 very consciously because we are vegan. Cats are carnivores and ours are fed as such. But, Howy's damaged pancreas was no longer able to properly process the B12 from his food. As a result, almost nothing got into his intestines and we had to supplement it in relatively large quantities.

The critical question was how we could get the B12 into Howy. I was told that you had to inject it, and taught how I could do it myself. OK, if I have to, I would learn.

I have to honestly say I wasn't comfortable at all with injections. Not because of the injection itself, but because Howy was so thin and I didn't want to hurt him. To make matters worse, B12 is particularly uncomfortable and burns quite a bit when injected. However, I managed to do it under the guidance of the vet!

Howy was to be given a small dose several times a week, later only once a week, and then as indicated. In a few weeks, we should have the B12 level checked again. Equipped with syringes, we ordered the vitamin B12 for him from the pharmacy. Now we could begin.

Theoretically, that is. In practice it wasn't so easy. Howy is a very agile tomcat that can be very slippery and proficient at evading you, squirming and turning really quickly. So he had to be held. We therefore planned for giving injections on the days when Cat Dad was at home. It was a real trial every time.

After a few times, I accidentally hurt him with the needle. In an attempt to avoid the syringe, he moved in exactly the wrong direction, toward the syringe instead of away from it. He complained loudly as it jabbed him. I would have too. I was so shocked, I was so sorry. It was my mistake, I should have reacted faster.

I connected with him a little later and explained everything to him, asking for his forgiveness. I never wanted to hurt him. He understood and forgave me. He just didn't want to be injected anymore. He had enough of that. I could certainly understand.

I dissolved the energetic blockage created by the shock of the needle accident, so that he wouldn't have problems at the vet. He accepted that process, and in all subsequent situations in which he needed an injection at the vet, we had no problem with it.

I promised him I would find another way to supplement vitamin B12. Even if the efficacy would be lower with an oral dose, some supplement would get absorbed. I explained this to Howy and asked him if he wanted to try it that way. Yes, he wanted that. He would lick it up even if it tasted nasty. It's so great that I learned to talk to animals!

So the problem was solved. From then on, I mixed the B12 from an ampoule with some cat cream on scheduled days, and Howy licked it up as discussed. I was really proud of him!

After six weeks I had the vitamin B12 level checked and what do you know: it was now in the upper reference range. And, his vomiting almost completely stopped. We were to continue giving him a maintenance dose every week from then on, and that worked very well.

In this situation, too, bioresonance was of great help and complemented conventional medical therapy perfectly. As soon as the B12 level rose again, Howy's body began to demand vitamin B6 and other B vitamins that his body could not convert. We fed those to him orally as well. Howy got quite fit again in terms of vitamins. And, the most important result for Howy: The vomiting was as good as gone!

Patchy's Departure and Her Cat Dwelling

Our friend Wally had to let her beloved Patchy go in early 2019 when she had just turned 22 years old. A truly proud age, considering that the cat had been a diabetic for over eleven years. She was lovingly and consistently supplied with her insulin and everything that such a senior cat needs. I had accompanied both of them energetically on their path. I was especially involved when the situation looked critical a few weeks earlier, because Patchy was having trouble urinating.

As you can imagine, with old animals it is not easy to see clearly whether they are simply going downhill or whether there is an acute problem, such as acute pain that requires immediate help. Wally wanted to do the right thing for Patchy, but found herself facing vets and therapists who no longer wanted to take a close look, and blamed everything on Patchy's age. Wally had no problem letting her cat go. She just wanted to give Patchy a fair chance in the best way possible and support her on her path.

An aura clearing for both of them removed blockages and brought tremendous clarity and strength to both Patchy and Wally. It was now apparent to Wally that she needed help managing Patchy's back pain that prevented her from urinating. Wally found the right help quickly and Patchy was able to eliminate by herself again. So, she didn't want to leave yet. There often are very subtle differences that need to be recognized. As caretakers, we owe it to our animals to be extremely observant.

I am describing this example here because it happens much too frequently in such situations that animals are prematurely "released from their suffering." It is important to assess carefully and to recognize whether it is an acute problem that needs to be addressed, or whether this is a signal that the animal wants to leave.

Patchy's trip to Rainbowland didn't take place until a few weeks later. What I want to tell you here has to do with Patchy's legacy. Patchy had a really nice, light-gray cat dwelling made of felt, with cuddly blankets inside. A few months after Patchy's death, when Wally was ready to part with this dwelling, she immediately thought of Flix. Like Patchy, Flix was a black and white cat—only half her size.

When I was on the way back from visiting my mother, I drove by Wally's place and picked up the nice dwelling with many thanks. As soon as I got home, I put it in the bedroom, where Flix had a little bed.

We couldn't expect that Boss Cat and persistent analyst Flix would immediately accept the new dwelling. It took a couple of days. He had to examine it from all sides first, and he smelled Patchy on it. He seemed to like that, because he spent a lot of time sniffing out the new cat dwelling.

In the meantime, Wally had spoken with Patchy, asking her to please persuade little Flix that the cat dwelling was meant for him. For him alone. I explained the same to Flix.

By the next day, he was inside the dwelling! How nice. Fantastic. He appeared so comfortable in it. From then on, the felt dwelling became his castle, his fortress. In the cooler months, he spent time inside almost every day and often much of the night. He could be found there most mornings when he was recovering from the stressful night patrols.

WALLY ON DUTY

We usually arranged our schedules in such a way that the few times I had to travel on business, Michael would do his work in his home office and take care of both cats. With Howy's and Flix's chronic issues, it was no longer feasible to have a cat sitter look after them.

We had set up this plan for the fall of 2019. I had three conferences on my schedule, two in England and one in the US. Then a great opportunity arose for me on very short notice. My teacher Toby invited me to a three-day workshop in Las Vegas on DNA activation and remote viewing, deepening the knowledge obtained in the courses I had taken over the previous years. As a complement to my previous studies, I definitely wanted to take advantage of this opportunity. However, Michael couldn't arrange his schedule to care for the cats, so I asked Wally. It worked out perfectly. She was able to come and stay for a few days that week to look after our two cats.

Wally is a Cat Mum through and through. She knew both our cats from previous visits and from the close exchanges that we have had for several years. The cats were in good shape, no current crises. I explained to the two of them via animal communication that they would be looked after by Wally at home; that she would live here so they could stay in their familiar surroundings. She would be there only a few days, from Monday lunchtime to Wednesday evening. Then Michael would come home, and I would be back on Friday morning.

Soul Cats

I was really looking forward to my trip, even though I still found it difficult to leave my cats at home. Often while sitting at the airport I would already be missing them tremendously. I got a little better at this over time. There was no reason to get stressed, as they couldn't be looked after any better.

Wally had the current food and medication plans and was well prepared. As always, we would exchange information via WhatsApp.

Howy was well adjusted and Flix was also in a good mood. He wasn't eating much the last few days, concentrating mainly on the chicken that was served in the evening. Well, he's had phases like that before. His fur looked pretty good, no kidney fur or anything like that.

I drove to the airport on Monday morning and Wally was on duty by noon. I had a pleasant trip, all flights were on time, that's the way I like it. During the stopover in Denver, Wally reported via WhatsApp. All is good, arrived safely. With Howy everything was great, he had eaten, only Flix didn't have an appetite. In the evening he ate more when there was fresh chicken. My little Flix ...

The next few days continued much the same as far as Flix's eating behavior was concerned. Wally thought something was wrong with him. Would he be reacting so sensitively because I wasn't there, and Wally was instead? I replied he was used to that, my mother-in-law had looked after them when we were on vacation in June, and they had coped well.

Howy, in any case, seemed to be enjoying Wally to the fullest, cuddling with her, entertaining her, and ending the day by disappearing into one of his cat tree hollows. Flix also joined in and made it clear that he liked her. If only there wasn't his lack of eating, which continued when Michael came back. Hmm. When I got home on Friday morning it was no different. He was happy that I was back, but, yes, something was wrong. I decided that I would watch him and see how Saturday went. Maybe he was just stressed out.

194

FLIX'S KIDNEY CRISIS, TAKE 2

Saturday didn't get any better, and neither did Sunday. Flix basically ate only half the usual amount of food. And he looked weak. It had nothing to do with me, something was wrong.

When he didn't touch his portion on Sunday evening, and looked to be very, very tired, it was clear what I had to do. Pack up the cat and drive to the clinic. I carried him down in his blanket and sat briefly on the sofa until Michael brought the cat carrier. Howy came to us, nudged him with his paw, as if to say "Hey buddy, I'm really sorry for that, all the best to you." Flix didn't even hiss at him. That clearly showed what bad shape he was in and how much he valued Howy's closeness.

I drove with him to the Hofheim Veterinary Clinic on Sunday evening. I was very nervous. Could it be an acute kidney crisis that had begun so insidiously that it was difficult to identify?

Flix was quiet, he said nothing. He hardly moved. He was really not doing well. It felt like he was showing how miserable he was.

We had to spend some time in the cat waiting room. I opened the door of his transport carrier so that I could comfort him better. We had to wait quite a while. Other people there also had animals that required emergency services.

Then it was our turn. The vet we saw didn't know Flix yet, but had already looked at his extensive patient file and knew what he was dealing with. He quickly came to the conclusion that I had suspected: acute kidney crisis. He explained to me that, ideally, Flix should stay in the clinic for a few days so that IV therapy could have the best effect. I connected to Flix's feelings and tried to figure out what he wanted. I explained to him what the vet's plan was. He wasn't enthusiastic about anything. He was far too nauseous. Well, let's try it.

In difficult situations, Flix tends to be sad and hide away, or he doesn't show interest in anything, or he becomes depressed. Both of us had experienced all of these reactions. But in this difficult situation, he would either have to stay at the clinic for a few days or risk his life. Well, it seemed necessary; we had everything else, including the vestibular syndrome, super under control.

So, with a heavy heart, I decided that Flix would stay in the clinic. I had to fly to London the next day for a keynote presentation on Tuesday. Michael was at home for Howy. Still, all this was causing me a major headache. I explained the situation to the vet. He said to go ahead, it wouldn't make sense to release Flix before Tuesday night anyway. They would call me every day. Yes, I already knew that. Alright, it couldn't be helped. If we wanted him to have a chance, we had to do it this way.

I took a lot of time saying goodbye to Flix, explained everything to him again, and asked him to be brave. I briefly explained to the staff his peculiarities, and how he would often hum to gain respect, but that now he was just afraid.

I completed the paperwork, and then the vet came out one more time and told me that the IV catheter had been inserted without any problems. Thank God! Usually that was very difficult ...

Going back home was all that I could do. Quite clearly. But leaving my overly sensitive Flix at the clinic was very difficult for me. He tended to internalize everything. Howy was different, he commented on everything immediately. The vets could tell much more about how things were going and how he was feeling. Max was the same. Not Flix. It was quite difficult to determine how Flix was really doing.

I flew to London the next day. At the airport, I got a call from the clinic that Flix was fine, that he was reacting well to his infusion and that he had already eaten on his own. Tomorrow they would check the kidney function levels and then decide whether he could go home yet. That sounded great!

I successfully completed my keynote on Tuesday morning and was heading back to the airport in the afternoon. The call from the clinic: Flix had eaten something, but his kidney function levels had not improved. They recommended keeping him there for another day so that he could continue to receive IV fluids. Hmm. That sounded reasonable.

I flew home thinking a lot about Flix on the way, sent him a lot of energy and promised him that I would bring him home tomorrow.

On Wednesday I waited for the call from the clinic. The ward doctor was pleased; Flix's kidney function levels were exceptionally good. What a relief! Soon he would be home to his familiar surroundings, and be able to recover from the stress. I got in the car right away to pick him up.

At the clinic they told me what he was allowed to have and what not. The vet wrote everything down in the original plan. Great, so I was able to hang this plan back up on the holder in the kitchen right after I returned home.

Then I waited for Flix to be brought to me. It took forever. I didn't have a good feeling. Removing the IV catheter and bandaging. That was it, wasn't it? When he was finally brought out to me, I was shocked. He was completely stressed; his eyes had an empty look. He sat in a very peculiar manner in his transport carrier; very strange. OK, we would cuddle a lot at home and everything would be fine.

I drove home with him. He tried changing position in the carrier several times, from right to left, from one side to the other. Something was wrong, but I couldn't see anything. The leg to which the IV catheter had been attached was bandaged. It was always like that.

When I got home, I opened the transport carrier and Flix stumbled out. He could hardly walk, dragged the leg to which the bandage was still attached, and could hardly put weight on that paw. I was horrified. What just happened? I had never received a cat back from the clinic in such bad condition. I somehow managed to get the bandage off him. He could still hardly put any weight on this leg. I carried him upstairs and thought he might want to go straight to his cave. No, he didn't want that. He teetered downstairs again, on only three legs. And where did he go? To the ground-level cave of the black scratching barrel.

I didn't have a good feeling. The last time he took refuge in this ground-level cave was right after his ear surgery in January 2017, when his polyp was removed. That was almost three years ago.

I put an orange blanket inside the cave. It seemed appropriate to me to use the color of the second chakra. He accepted it immediately. I prepared something for him to eat and cat cream and filled his water bowl. It wasn't going to be easy. His eyes were telling me everything. He was completely exhausted.

Don't Eat, Stay in the Cave

I called the veterinary clinic, desperate to know what had happened. It was clear to me that something unusual had occurred. Flix's condition was just too terrible. I explained exactly what bothered me, and that I had never received a cat back in this condition from the clinic.

I wanted to work energetically with Flix and resolve any trauma. All I needed to know was what happened while he was there. And no, he wasn't simply stressed. He was completely off track. Why could he barely walk? Because of the IV catheter? I think not. They knew me well there. They knew that I was careful and not one of those hysterical, fear-driven animal owners. Yeah, I really needed a call back. Yes, today.

When the vet called back, I described Flix's condition and said that he hadn't eaten anything, absolutely nothing. And, he could still hardly step on the hind leg, where the bandage was.

It turned out that Flix had removed the first IV catheter himself, which was in a front leg. Ouch! Then fate took its course because he had to get a new IV catheter in the back, the left hind leg. And he hated that. Especially since he probably had an old injury on the left backside, as we had found out in an earlier animal communication. But you couldn't see it, and the veterinary clinic wasn't aware of it. And I hadn't pointed it out ...

To make matters worse, he didn't really want to cooperate with removing it. He just had enough. The adhesive tape that was used tugged too much on his leg and the joint, which of course wasn't in good shape at his advanced age either. Removing the catheter probably caused this pain. OK, understood. Why they had to put the pressure bandage on so tight, however, will remain a mystery to me personally.

I thanked them for their honesty. I appreciated that because I know how it works in emergency services; that callbacks are not usual. I wanted to start working energetically with Flix to resolve what had happened, but he didn't want that. Whenever you work energetically with a living being, you ask for permission. You can then feel by the flow of energy whether it is a yes or a no. This was a no. Actually, it was a "not yet," as I later realized.

So, I had my Flix back with great kidney function levels, but totally exhausted, totally stressed out. Traumatized. I was afraid that he would give up now. He stayed in his cave, didn't eat anything. He went to his drinking stations several times and drank quite a bit. At least he did that.

I decided to let him first do exactly what he wanted to do. Don't eat anything, stay in the cave. I had set up a small buffet for him in front of the cave, with different types of food, cat cream, and kidney tonic.

The next morning, I found that he had eaten absolutely nothing. But, he must have continued to drink water. Well, that was something. He lingered in his dark cave, came out only to drink. Afterwards he looked around once or twice and that was it. Back into the cave.

On Thursday, I offered him all kinds of food alternatives. Still he ate nothing. He looked at his buffet but was very clear in his decision: "No, I don't want anything."

His hind leg did improve, however. He could move it almost normally. I was very happy. I wasn't sure what he was trying to say to me with his behavior. Was he so traumatized that he just needed time? Did he mean to tell me that he'd rather leave? Or had he slipped into a depression again due to all the stress in the clinic, and everything around him was dark and terrible, without any light at the end of the tunnel?

Whatever it was, he had to start eating again. To go for such a long time, almost 40 hours, without eating anything, was very bad and might already have caused some liver damage. I knew that. Still, I felt it was wrong to force food on him. In the evening, I tried again to dissolve the trauma energetically. No, he didn't allow it. It is extremely rare for a soul to say "No, I don't want that now." And it was the first and only time that Flix's soul signaled this so clearly. Usually, he gratefully accepted any energetic help that was offered to him. For me this was a sign of how great his despair, his trauma, and his stress were.

On Friday morning, he had his Skype appointment with Tom. Ever since Tom had moved his practice to Saarland, he looked after Howy and Flix via Skype. Tom examined Flix via bioresonance and received back a catastrophic psychological state. That was exactly what I had felt, too. The stress of the clinic routine and the issue of the IV catheter led to a depression that he wouldn't necessarily beat on his own. Not quickly enough, anyway. So he was treated with an appropriate bioresonance program and psychologically stabilized.

At about the same time, our regular vet called from the clinic and inquired about Flix. Both Tom and the vet said the same thing: he has to eat again. And right away, or the risks of organ damage would be too great. I understand this problem. Still, it was important that Flix was heard. The vet explained to me that very old cats suffered in particular from being in the hospital, and that they always went home very stressed, even if there were no special incidents. And, Flix experienced all those stresses. He didn't like changes anyway. Now he had to overcome special incidents. Surely, he remembered his stay at the clinic three years ago, when everything was spinning around him and he was fighting for his life. So, a lot came together for him as his world was again collapsing.

We fed him by syringe. Recovery formula, mixed with some water; we put it into the syringe, wrapped a towel around him, one person held him while the other fed him. When he allowed this to be done to him without complaint, I was relieved. It had all been way too much for Flix; he needed help on his way back to life. He didn't want to leave. Had that been the case, he would not have let us feed him. Then he gradually got better.

Throughout Friday, he allowed me to energetically clear the trauma from the clinic. I felt it strongly when that clumped energy cleared inside him. At last! A very important step on the way to recovery. He looked different again. His eyes slowly regained their clarity and radiance. This took a gigantic load off my mind!

He started pacing his territory again. He had relinquished it all to Howy during his illness. Although Howy took care of it, he was a stranger to Flix's meticulousness in everything. He handled it in a much more relaxed way.

Flix slowly recovered. He started eating again. He was getting better every day. He moved into his cat dwelling in the bedroom and soon grew back into his role of Boss Cat.

Howy was so wonderful to Flix when he came home from the clinic. No bickering because he smelled of clinic, nothing at all. No hissing because he had made himself comfortable in the living area downstairs. Howy was just there with all of his positive energy and love for Flix. Quite marvelous. He gave him space to find himself again.

Howy was worried about Flix; it was obvious. He stayed more in the background and helped just with his energy and his presence. Flix could be Flix with all his idiosyncrasies. Howy let him do everything and helped him, by sharing his own love and joy of life, to slowly find his way back into life.

ENDING THE YEAR 2019

I only had one conference scheduled in Chicago in November. It was my last business trip this year. But, the day before I was due to leave, something happened that left me in a state of crisis.

The company I worked for had been sold. We had known about it for a long time, and the deal was implemented in November. In the weeks before, my uneasy feeling increased that this deal was not as strategic as we had been assured. What happened was something that I had suspected for weeks, but did not want to admit. The research department for which I worked as Research Director was hit to the core. All analysts, including myself, were told they would no longer be needed. A "package" detailing my compensation for terminating my contract would be sent to me. I should stay until the end of the year to process client orders. Then my notice period would take effect.

I received this information one hour before I left for the airport. Phew. Even though I suspected it, being informed in this way was painful. I had enjoyed my role and had created a lot of added value for many clients and companies. None of that was needed anymore, said the new owner. Well, that's how things work. At the end of the day, as an employee, you have relatively little influence. A tough but educational experience.

I told Flix what I had just heard. He sensed my stress. And his look was so precious; I had never seen him with this expression before. "What? They're terminating you? Are they crazy?"

I flew to Chicago and gave a brilliant keynote presentation that was very well received. I really wanted to leave a great final mark. This was important for me. Especially because I wasn't able to talk to anyone about it yet.

I would have to organize myself anew. Find new paths for me and embark on them. From my current perspective, more than six months later, I can say that it was meant to be. I needed this push to restructure and set up differently both my energetic work and my consulting work for companies. A common denominator had to be found. There was a lot of work waiting for me. Especially relating to myself.

When I was back home and everything could settle a bit, I realized that Flix and Howy felt exactly what was wrong with me, what troubled me, how hurt I was inside—and how much I needed this restart at the same time.

During the animal conversations I had with both of them over the following weeks, it became clear how much they both sensed what was going on, and how much trust they had in me. Both saw it as a necessary upheaval, as an opportunity to get involved and develop in a completely different way. Both of them had already developed clarity about it that I only recognized much later.

Our animals perceive everything that happens in our lives. And they carry it all with us and for us. Max says a little more from his point of view in the chapter "Max On Animal Souls and Human Souls."

That is exactly what I want to address here. What our animals carry for us puts a strain on their souls and ultimately also on their bodies.

What I learned through my energetic work, with regard to aura and karma clearing, is this: Everything that shows up as a physical symptom has existed for a long time as a blockage in the energy field, in the aura. In animals as in humans. The book *Vibrational Medicine*[1] opened my eyes to it; and even more so did Toby Alexander, my teacher from whom I learned these clearing techniques.

So, I dedicated myself to staying as free as possible from energetic blockages, just like I did with our cats. Weekly aura clearing sessions for the whole family became the norm. It was very good for all of us. I really wanted to make sure the cats weren't dealing with anything more than they had already brought with them. Of course I wanted to keep both of us humans

---

1. Richard Gerber, MD: *Vibrational Medicine*, Bear & Co., 2001, ISBN 978-1-87918-158-8.

energetically as clear as possible, so that we had full access to our vital life energy at all times, free of any blockages.

This was the beginning of a wonderful path which helped me advance, and also clearly showed me that the cats benefited from it. Mentally and physically. Our vet often said that they were little medical miracles, especially when you consider how Flix needed to learn everything all over again after his surgery. Now a completely new Flix had been created. Since that time, he has grown beyond any expectations. And that was over three years ago!

Also, look at Howy! His life was already on the brink in the first six weeks he was with us, and we managed several subsequent crises, attacks of pancreatitis and biliary congestion. More than once, a vet would tell me: "You know Howy is a very, very old cat." Yes, of course I know. Age is relative. What the animals want, where they are on their life's journey, that is the decisive factor. That's why we still helped him as long as he wanted to live. Each time around, the vets treating him were surprised by Howy's temperament and fighting spirit. Many factors were at play. Energetic work also had a role that should not be underestimated for both cats.

This is how we ended 2019. A phase of life came to an end for me. It was important to use my skills and to translate the topics that were close to my heart into meaningful offerings for companies and individuals.

An important ritual was the creation of an annual photo book that chronicled the lives of the two cats in pictures over the past year. This was a process that I thoroughly enjoyed and that often opened my eyes in retrospect, giving me insight into how the two of them were doing. It also showed what we had mastered together, how we had grown individually.

As always, New Year's Eve was a stressful time for Flix. Howy didn't hear well anymore, so he dealt better with New Year's Eve noise. Only Flix had an issue with it. He was very scared. Still, it showed how much more trust he had developed over time. Years before he had crawled under the dresser in the hall days before New Year's Eve, as soon as the blasting noise of the first firecrackers could be heard.

This year he was brave. It wasn't until New Year's Eve itself that he became a little restless. After two hours of fireworks, he was very scared. But he came to us, I took him in my arms and we survived that, too.

A new year was just around the corner! 2020!

HOWY PREPARES HIS DEPARTURE

Howy started the new year with different routines. From my current perspective, I know that he deliberately ushered in the last phase of his life with us.

He would consciously approach Flix over and over again. He expanded this behavior further, and now went up to Flix in the bedroom, visiting for entire afternoons. Both cats then spent the afternoon together. Howy snuggled into one of the many pillows on the bed, and Flix mostly stayed in his cat dwelling he got as a gift from Patchy.

I am sure that both of them had wonderful cat conversations. Beyond our perceptual capability. On a different wavelength. They usually seemed very peaceful. Each of them in his own world, but still together. Our senior residential community!

It became more noticeable that Howy was the first to go to bed in the evening—that is into our bed. Most of the time before that, he ended our evenings by jumping off the sofa and then walking over to his cat tree, snuggling up in the mid-level perch. That meant "Good night" and "You can now go to bed too!" Sure, Howy, we will!

He now had changed this behavior; he went upstairs to our bed and waited there for his humans to follow him. Most of the time when I was alone during the week, Howy snuggled up next to me at pillow level and fell asleep there. When Michael was home, Howy parked himself in between our pillows. Being with his humans now seemed to have become even more important to him. It was beautiful and so peaceful to feel Howy next to me.

Flix obviously had no issue with it. He handled it in his own way. Since Howy was upstairs at night, someone had to watch out for everything downstairs. So Boss Cat Flix usually stayed downstairs and watched over that area. To do this, he marched through the apartment like a security guard, round after round, hour after hour. He usually didn't come back into the upstairs bedroom until the early hours of the morning when Howy went downstairs. They had arranged it very precisely. So everything went quite smoothly.

Howy's body was now gradually deteriorating. He ate a little less. Sometimes he couldn't bring himself to eat until the evening. Then he ate more at night, which was OK because we knew him to be a night eater. In total, however, Howy ate less and less. And he lost weight. It was difficult to maintain his 5.5 lbs.

He stopped climbing up all the way to the top of the cat tree. Up to his cave, yes, he did that until the end, but he slowly stopped climbing up to the next level onto the upper perch.

From mid-April on, he was given an appetite stimulator every now and then. We had this emergency remedy available if he didn't want to eat for more than a day. Our vet had instructed us when and how much he should get.

He caught up a whole day's eating when we used it; he ate his meals with appetite and joy. As always, bite by bite and spread out over the day, rather than the night. At some point, we took his food to bed with us to make sure that he could eat wherever he was. But his eating didn't get better, it got worse. It could not go on like that. We needed help. When he couldn't use the litter box in early May, Tom helped remotely via bioresonance. Tom found that the intestines were pressing on the stomach, so nothing would come out the colon. Howy didn't want to eat anything because of the stomach pressure. We first helped with Lactulose to aid defecation and give him relief. He was able to use the litter box again the next day. But he wasn't really feeling any better.

On Monday, May 11th, he was so limp and ill that I drove straight to the clinic with him. There he was examined in the emergency service. Nothing could be seen on the X-ray because his tummy was filled with an indefinable liquid. An ultrasound was done, but most of the organs could no longer be delimited. He had this liquid throughout his lower abdomen. And, his liver cysts had changed dramatically in a matter of months, after this hadn't bothered him for nearly three years. There was a lot out of balance. A needle aspiration was performed to examine the fluid in his abdomen. Lots of bacteria, but no cancer cells could be found.

Howy received an injection of Cerenia for the nausea and vitamin B12, and then we drove home. The emergency service vet wanted to discuss with our regular vet whether or not he could be supported with cortisone.

Our vet called me late at night, expressing dismay at how fast Howy's condition had deteriorated. She wanted us to come back the next day to take a blood sample. Without that, she could not make the decision about possible cortisone therapy. So, Howy and I went back to the clinic the next day. Howy used to be talkative in the car. Especially in city traffic, he commented on every stop and start. He was quieter now. He had no problem going back to Hofheim the next day. He knew our vet. It was nothing new to him. Howy's blood was easy to draw before. Not that day. It didn't really want to flow. Howy endured the time-consuming procedure without any problems. He knew nobody wanted to hurt him. As always, he commented on what had happened during the consultation. The vet notes usually said "lively, attentive."

As expected, his blood inflammation levels were astronomical and unfortunately his neutrophils were very low. Our vet examined him again and looked at all the findings from the previous day. Septic abdomen, which already caused fluid to build up in the abdominal cavity. So, we could not support him with cortisone therapy, which could at least stabilize and contain what was happening. Cortisone was an immunosuppressant, and combined with the already low neutrophils would probably shut down his immune system. Instead, she advised me to give him an antibiotic. It was one that he had already received, and would get the infectious process in his abdomen under control, at least temporarily.

We drove home with a new medication regimen: the antibiotic twice a day, the medication that regulated biliary stasis, vitamin B12, his medicinal mushrooms, Cerenia for another three days, and whenever necessary the appetite stimulator—at most every second, better every third day. He should keep getting his CBD oil, which had been effective at pain relief for several months. With CBD he no longer had any more colicky pain.

IT'S THE LITTLE MOMENTS
THAT COUNT

A nimals know exactly what to expect and what phase of their incarnation
they are in. They handle themselves very consciously—and also their
humans, about whom they usually worry more than about themselves. If
you go through these phases with your senior animals consciously, you will
be richly gifted. We felt so gifted with Max and now with Howy.

Howy had a red cat bed with orange pillows. It came from our friend
Ellen from Schleswig-Holstein as a present for Howy. You remember that
she helped me a lot with Howy's integration. I had already worked energetically with some of her cats. When Howy got it, he was blown away and
it was his absolute favorite place for a couple of weeks. But then, from one
day to the next, he no longer cared about it.

Now spring was just around the corner, and during sunny weather we
had our breakfast on the loggia. Howy wanted to be there, this year too.
He came out with me, jumped on the bench and from there onto the table,
where he usually sat in the sun.

Now I had the idea to put the red cat bed on the loggia table for him
so that he was comfortable, softly supported and sheltered from the wind.
At the same time he could enjoy the morning sun.

He thought that was great. He accepted the bed on the table. In general,
he liked to be on the loggia, even in shady or windy weather. Even in earlier
years, he had already chosen the bench and slept on it for hours.

We could see how much he enjoyed the time with us in the morning sun. Since the bed had a rather high edge, which generated too much shade, I cut off the edge without further ado. And, I put another blanket on the pillows so that he was comfortable.

In early May, one day before the clinic trip with Howy for emergency service, we had our first visit from dear friends for Sunday breakfast since the coronavirus lockdown. Howy was very happy. He was already there to help me set the table in his tried and tested way, which meant that he commented loudly on what I was doing, and stood exactly where I wanted to put something! And, he insisted on running across the table, sitting on Cat Dad's lap, sitting on our friends Beate and Michael's laps, and proudly sitting between them. He enjoyed this visit, although he was not doing very well. It was Sunday when we finally got his digestion going again and were actually hoping that things would continue to improve.

Howy also had his last bioresonance appointment outside on the loggia in the sunlight a few days later. He made himself comfortable on the orange pillow in front of the bed. I placed my laptop in front of it so that Tom could see that Howy was in control.

May was very sunny, actually much too warm and dry. It was nice for Howy; he could start the day with us almost every morning. It's the little moments that you never forget ...

For lunch, if it wasn't too hot, we moved to the balcony, which due to the large tree in front of the house turned into a kind of tree garden. The balcony is much narrower, it only fits a small table and two of the garden chairs; but that's of course because we have eleven flower pots there.

Howy loved sitting on Cat Dad's lap. Or to sit on the lawn chair. Like Max before. And like we did with Max, one of us often sat in the balcony door on our folding chair so as not to disturb Howy.

Unlike Max, he loved to go from one human to the other across the table and sit down in our laps. Idyllic moments with Howy that nobody can take away from us and that we will forever carry in our hearts.

And of course the sofa moments with Cat Dad. That was something very special, Howy and his Cat Dad on the sofa. He loved to lie in the crook of Michael's arm and snuggled up closely to him. Often they were lying on the sofa for hours and Cad Dad fell asleep before Howy did ...

LETTING GO

Clearing energetic blockages is one of my favorite pastimes, and I had become highly skilled in doing it. Although I provided it primarily for humans, the same methods were also effective on our animals.

Both Howy and Flix were familiar with it: the clearing of one's own energy field, the aura, of everything that doesn't belong there. Both also knew karma clearing, the removal of energetic blockages that we have either created ourselves, consciously or subconsciously, or that we inherited from our genetic parents at the time of conception and fetal integration. Put simply, all the issues that our parents did not resolve for themselves are transferred directly to us into our DNA. It's the same with our animals.

Especially during Howy's last few weeks, I tuned myself into his feelings every day to see whether something had to be cleared, and if so what. With Howy, the issues of guilt and shame kept coming up over and over again. And also limitations. Deeper and deeper levels, mostly from previous lives. All of that accompanied him throughout this life. He gratefully accepted the clearing. In this life he was focused on being able to let go of it all. Who is surprised that he came to us, especially to me? I could provide excellent help with that.

Although Howy had physically manifested various blockages, we managed to keep these events under control for a long time, and reliably so. After each flare-up, the vets were thrilled that his pancreas was still working.

Its limited functionality had hardly deteriorated. We were able to stabilize everything, including the liver cysts. They hadn't bothered him for nearly three years, and remained stable until almost exactly six weeks before he died. Then the situation changed markedly and everything around it spiraled out of control. That's the physical perspective. Energetically, his soul prepared itself to leave his body behind.

THEY ONLY MOVE

Even though in my energetic work I now focus on aura clearing and karma clearing, as well as DNA activation and reading the Akashic Records, I use animal communication with my animals only for "regular use at home." This is because I have learned that with my own animals, especially when the situation is critical and I am emotionally involved, I prefer to ask someone else to talk to them.

So I asked my dear friend Kerstin, who specialized in animal communication, to accompany Howy on this last journey.

On May 20th, she received this information from him:

Dear Tamara,
Just spoke to Howy.

Body feelings:
The hind legs feel weak. I feel slight muscle twitches and a tingling sensation in the back paws. I feel hungry but no appetite. The thought of food makes me feel sick. I feel extremely thirsty. Mint immediately comes to my mind. The smell and taste are so good ...

I cannot feel any direct pain. Except for headaches, but I had them before.

Howy knows how things are with him and he accepts it as well. He seems completely clear and very relaxed again.

He says that when the time comes to leave, it'll be perfectly fine.

He says *"I'm very lucky, I'm heard and understood, and I know I'm allowed to leave. I am allowed to walk in the love that has always surrounded me and I take this love with me, forever. I am infinitely grateful to be able to experience that."*

I ask Howy what his wishes are. Howy wants to go home. He would like to determine it himself and experience it consciously. But he is not sure whether or not you can cope with walking this path with him. His wish is not to be alone when the time comes ...

He enjoys every moment and the physical closeness provides him with support and trust. And it should give you strength. He always feels how you are doing.

"No matter how much time we have left, let's just enjoy it ... now and here."

I'm sitting here in the grass and the birds are chirping while I talk to Howy. During his last comment, the sun suddenly comes out for a short moment between all the clouds that were there all day today.

———————

Yes, that's the way animals are. Even when they are not doing well themselves, they worry about their humans. Dear Howy, we will walk with you on your path the way you want us to, of course. Our animals are so full of love. To be able to accompany them on their last journey is very intense, very beautiful, unforgettable, and such a great gift; and so much love remains. With us. Between us. For us. With us.

I've already seen it with Max. If we consciously accompany them to the end, we receive more than is supposedly taken away from us by their departure. They're just moving to another place. To an apartment beyond the horizon. They are still there. Their energy, their love. In our hearts. If we allow it. When we learn to navigate with the heart instead of just the head, then we continue to feel them. How they accompany us.

The most important thing in these processes is to keep the heart open, not to close it. Only open hearts can experience, feel, and receive love.

The conversation fit wonderfully with my perception of Howy. Regarding his sensitive awareness, his openness, his wisdom, his clarity, his love.

We spent the next few days with a lot of awareness, to see how we could help him. What he would like to experience. And how.

We had intense moments in the morning at breakfast when he was with us on the loggia. When he was on the balcony at lunchtime, to join us when we ate lunch or drank coffee. It was about the moments that we had with him, and that he had with us. That was wonderful. Howy taught me again what it means to be in the here and now. To accept what is. In gratitude. In love.

This is one of the core topics that I work on for myself. Animals are great teachers to us, if we let them. If we accept what they want to show and teach us. Deep inside of us. Accept it in our heart.

So these weeks were naturally very intense, no question about it, and also wonderful. You learn the most in life when you have to get out of your comfort zone. Being able to accompany an animal on its last journey in life is never a comfort zone. It takes our entire being to navigate with the heart. Because there are no blueprints, no right or wrong, because every process of every animal is highly individual. Just as this last path is unique for each person. There is no such thing as "that's how it works" and "that's right" or "that's wrong." We have to find our common path, ideally always guided by the thought that we need to enable our animals to take the path they wish to take.

On Wednesday, May 27th, I asked Kerstin again to look after him:

"Hello dear Kerstin!

"Would you please check back in and talk to Howy?

"He is very brave, but he also seems very withdrawn since today. He doesn't want to eat today.

"The black mass—he had developed a black scab on his nose—fell off yesterday ... as if he were letting go of what he no longer needed.

"The day before yesterday, he fell from the cat tree while jumping up. His jumping power is decreasing and his muscles are getting weaker. He got back on his paws and today he was up there again! Incredible, the little fighter.

"Would you see again what he is thinking, and what he would like? And is he in pain anywhere?

"THANK YOU from the bottom of my heart!"

That was Wednesday, which was the turning point for me, the turning point toward the actual dying process.

Kerstin received this from him on May 28th:

I have a hard time connecting with Howy today. Took a couple of attempts. In contrast to other times when I always see the animals first and only then perceive their body feelings; with Howy it is so that I can't see him today but only feel him.

Body feelings:
Right at the beginning of our connection, a tingling sensation flows through my entire body. The chest feels very hot for a moment, but it is not an uncomfortable feeling. The hind legs appear very shaky and powerless.

My eyes are starting to water ...

The abdomen feels cramped. As if everything contracts inward.

I still can't see him and I ask him why. Why he doesn't want to show himself today.

For a brief moment, I suddenly see him, sitting upright on a bright, narrow surface. A windowsill?

He looks so happy and satisfied while doing it.

He says *"You can trust me,"* and I hear the word trust as an echo a couple of times ...

Then he's gone again ...

My tears start flowing again ...

This was my answer:

"Dear Kerstin! First of all, thank you very much!!!

"Today was kind of a turning point. He has not eaten anything and strictly refuses to accept his medication. He came out on our balcony for lunch, very consciously enjoyed the sun, but was somehow different. Then he went into the cave and only recently came out.

"I suppose when he came out he was 'gone' with you. I have the feeling that we won't have much time left ... will now try to give him some recovery food so that he can get some liquid. His little face has changed a lot today.

"Yes, the hind legs are wobbly. He leans against the litter box to not fall.

"He is now using his climbing aids. It is very exhausting for him. But he wants to do it all himself.

"I feel that he doesn't want to say anything because he is afraid that I would have something else done that he doesn't want ... but we won't do that. Well, we're now just moving from one moment to the next ...

"THANK you from the bottom of my heart."

These days were very intense, but also wonderful. I know from numerous conversations with animals that many animals are afraid that their caretakers will still have something "done," even if their souls have already started on their path. This process takes a long time. For us humans, only the last phase is often really visible, when a human tangibly moves toward the physical end.

The more you succeed in listening to your heart and following your intuition, the sooner you will receive the right signals from your animal and be able to act accordingly. We are, so to speak, "process managers" on behalf of our animals. It is the last service of love that we can provide to them: to accompany and enable this process in the way that our animals want for themselves, as far as it is in our power.

For that, one thing is extremely important: to make it clear to the animal that it can leave, that everything is fine, that it does not have to worry about humans. Usually, the animal has fought for a long time to be able to stay here for us—because of us. So, it is very important that you convey to your animal that it can leave the way it wants to. That you understand. That you are grateful for the wonderful time you had together. That you will of course miss it a lot and cry a lot, but that is also part of the process.

Howy had known these things at the time. He knew that he would be heard, that he could leave, and that it would all be fine. Of course, the animal is also very attached to its life with us and will miss us. In this respect, it is important to take the time to say goodbye. Everything works out the way it should.

Going from resistance to acceptance is often the most difficult thing for us humans; not only on this topic. Accepting the way things are gives us the energy to go through the process with our animals.

You Can't Delegate Responsibility

It is not only important for humans to say goodbye to friends and companions whenever possible in the last weeks and days of their lives. It's important for animals, too.

For Howy, those humans he needed to say goodbye to include my mother-in-law Anneliese and my friend Wally, who both knew him well and had also looked after him. Then it was my dear friend Martina, who introduced him to us through the Hanau Animal Shelter, where we got to know him. And of course Kerstin and Kristin, who both talked to him and worked with him; and Ellen, who was always on hand to give us advice and assistance. And many more. Not all of them managed to see him personally, but all of them took the opportunity to say goodbye in their own way.

Wally managed to see him about two weeks before he died. Howy knew her well and he enjoyed spending time with her again. He knew she was coming to say goodbye to him.

It was sunny and we went out on the balcony. Howy followed directly behind us. He wanted to show her that he could still jump on the lawn chair himself. He was happy that Wally came to visit him. Then he sat with her on the sofa, cuddled with her; very important. When she was leaving later, she spoke to him directly, telling him that everything would be fine, that everything would go according to his wishes. He listened to her carefully.

And seriously. And calmly. At peace with himself. He knew what this was about.

Unfortunately, he could no longer meet with my mother-in-law. All of this happened when COVID-19 was raging, and at her age she was in one of the risk groups; so this was simply not an option for her.

Our dear friend Martina, who introduced him to us and had visited us and Howy several times, unfortunately just missed Howy. When I told her about his condition ten days before his death, she said she would visit the following weekend. But, she wasn't able to see him once more. He passed away on Saturday morning and she planned to come in the afternoon. I explained to him that Martina would still come. He understood, but the soul chooses its own path and time. I visited Martina a few weeks later and we talked about "our" wonderful Howy over coffee and cake. Of course he joined us spiritually. So it was all good.

Before Max's death, it had also been important that Max and Flix could say goodbye to each other. This made it a lot easier for Flix to deal with things and Max could calmly go on his way.

At the time, I was very grateful that the vets in the veterinary clinic saw it the same way. Yes, animals must be able to say goodbye. It is important to deal with these topics in advance, when you are not emotionally involved, when you can objectively consider options, possibilities, and approaches.

It is so enriching, for yourself and your animal, when you consciously walk this path, consciously experience it, experience it together. You can cope more easily with the fact that nobody is eyeing your food on the table anymore; that nobody is commenting loudly or snuggling in bed with you. All of this is much easier if you accompany them consciously.

Therefore, my urgent appeal to all those who may not yet have experienced the death of an animal or who are afraid of it: There is no reason to be afraid. It is a process during which you can grow a lot; that will enrich you tremendously.

Here is something very, very important. It is the *responsibility* that we took on for our animal the moment it moved in with us. From this moment on, the life of the animal depends on the decisions of its humans. You cannot give up that responsibility, especially not at the last moment of its life. Responsibility means not leaving them alone but accompanying them on their terms, as we would wish for ourselves.

Just show compassion. Let love speak. Then it becomes clear that we need to accompany our animals on their last journey over the Rainbow Bridge; that we are with them and hold their paws or their heads. With love. Connected to them. Respectfully. Responsibly. Infinitely grateful.

HOWY'S JOURNEY TO RAINBOWLAND

It started on Wednesday evening, May 27th. Howy decidedly rejected his antibiotic. He spat it out several times along with the empty capsule. OK, I understand, dear Howy. You don't want it anymore. So let's leave it. He took his recovery formula with CBD oil and B12. I could easily deliver it into his mouth with a syringe.

This Wednesday was the last day he ate anything worth mentioning. After that he stopped eating altogether. He was now a lot shakier. We put a stool in front of the bed, which he accepted with thanks. He really wanted to sleep with us at night and also be with Flix in the afternoon.

He first ignored the stool that we put next to the cat tree days ago, and then only used it to get down from it. It was only in the very last days of his life that he accepted this help for getting up as well. He was thin, lacked muscle strength, and since he ingested nothing except some water and some nutrients, his hind legs became quite wobbly.

On Thursday he tried very hard to keep up his routines. He still some-how managed to climb the cat tree and go into his beloved cave. And, he still managed to climb the stairs and curl up on the bed. He wanted to spend time with Flix and he wanted to sleep with us in the evening. It was very intense on both days as he snuggled up close to one of us, always alternating so that we could all feel his love. He went downstairs again at night, and in the morning he was in his favorite bed by the red pillar with a sculpture on top.

It was on Thursday that I searched for mobile vets. Howy's departure was imminent and I didn't want to have to drive around with him if we needed help. I found a mobile vet. I tried to call just to discuss the procedure in advance. But, nobody picked up the phone. Interestingly enough, no one called back either. From an energetic point of view, very clear: It wasn't supposed to happen.

On Friday, I felt that things were different. He continued to struggle to keep up his routines. He tried not to let it show. But he was weak and I expected a clear signal from his side that it was time to get help.

He was in his cave in the evening and made no move to come out. Should we leave him there? In the event that he wanted to leave peacefully, that would be perfectly suitable for him. But if that wasn't the case and he needed help, the cave was inconvenient. So what do we do?

There was a square piece of pelt on the bottom of the cave. As he was sitting on the pelt, it seemed actually pretty easy to get Howy out. For a moment, I tuned into his feelings and also concentrated on mine. Then it was clear: we will get him out. He had positioned himself in such a way that Michael could remove him relatively easily with the pelt underneath. I picked him up and offered him his evening formula with the CBD oil. He didn't want that anymore. Half of it spilled on him, so immediately I had to clean Howy off. All good now. I took him upstairs and put him on the bed. He liked that. When we went to bed, he snuggled up close to me; I stroked and hugged him, spoke calming words to him. Everything will be fine, dear Howy, it is your path and we will accompany you. Please tell us if you would like help. He then snuggled up to his Cat Dad.

We fell asleep, but woke up sometime early in the night to find Howy making his way downstairs. Michael went downstairs with him and slept on the sofa. He told me in the morning that Howy had rearranged his sleeping position by himself two more times.

When I woke up in the morning and went downstairs, Howy was sitting in one of the ground-level caves. I looked at him and it was clear. His eyes were a long way away. He was not doing well. The Howy laugh was no longer in his eyes. Now the moment had come.

I called the mobile vet. My call was answered immediately. I described the situation. She would be with us in half an hour. Wonderful.

Howy dragged himself out of the cave and lay down in his favorite bed by the red pillar. From then on, we didn't leave his side. Now I was crying big tears. I had to pull myself together; I wanted to be strong for him. I could cry later. Everything was easier said than done.

We both sat with him, stroked him, talked to him. The vet arrived much more quickly than expected. She examined him briefly, listened to our report and stated what we already knew. He was dying; he was already on his way. He would appreciate a bit of help on the last mile.

So, it was right to help him at this point. She explained the procedure to us, attached an IV catheter to him and started the anesthesia. Howy relaxed, I had his head in my hands, and built a pillow support under it because he let it hang out of the bed. I stabilized him that way.

A certain feeling of well-being came over me, of peace, of letting go. Then Howy's soul was gone and his little heart stopped beating.

As sad as it was, it was also beautiful and intense. We were able to accompany him, let him go in love, and had found exactly the right vet who carried the process out very lovingly. It couldn't have been done with more compassion. And in his favorite bed too. At home. With both of us at his side. That was what he wanted.

Howy was born sometime in 2001. In 2017 he was rescued by the fire brigade and given to the Hanau Animal Shelter. Apparently his caretaker had died. His illnesses were discovered in the animal shelter. We met him on July 19th at the Hofheim Veterinary Clinic. On July 29th, we visited him at the shelter. We adopted him on July 31st, 2017. He left this life on May 30th, 2020. A proud 19 years old, of which he had spent almost three years with us.

Even though these last weeks had been exhausting, they were also intense and beautiful, intimate and clear, honest and full of love.

We put his favorite things in his little bed, covered him with a cozy blanket, put his energy circle on top and added his rose quartz, which he always had in his cave. His energy circle was a photograph of symbol cards and minerals in a circle that Howy had chosen during animal communication. We kept it under his cat bed before. We added the maple leaf that was blowing on the balcony that morning, and an almost dried red peony. We kept him with us for 24 hours to make sure that his soul could go in peace, and that Flix could also say goodbye to him in peace.

Our beloved Howy had brought so much love and joy into all of our lives that the tears we shed for his death felt like drops in an ocean.

FLIX, THE REAL HERO

My little Flix, my dear Flix, it wasn't easy for him. For the second time, he had to let go of a beloved friend. More than three years ago Max left, and now Howy.

Max had saved his life when he took him, the sad, outcast Flix, under his wing in the animal shelter. And, because Max had made sure that we both adopted them. Now Howy had left, whom our dear Max had chosen for us—and especially for Flix.

At first it didn't look like Flix and Max would become friends. Flix was apparently not used to having a feline partner around. Max was someone completely different than Flix, on a completely different level, a real partner cat. Flix admired Max and fully recognized him as his Boss Cat and soul friend.

Flix's big moment came after Max's death and following his vestibular syndrome surgery. Everything was at stake and everything changed for him at the same time. For one thing, he had to get over Max's death, and, from now on, he had to make all feline decisions on his own. He also had a lot more work guarding his territory. In addition, after his vestibular syndrome surgery, he had to learn almost everything anew, such as walking, using the litter box, playing, mastering the stairs ...

So, in his old age, Flix suddenly had to become a Boss Cat, probably for the first time in his life. He had to relearn fundamental things. And then, as soon as he had everything under control again and had taken on his boss role, he had to come to terms with his new feline partner and make friends. Not an easy task for a serious, deep, analytical, always very reflective tomcat.

For a long time, it looked as if Flix would tolerate Howy rather than like him. It turned out, however, that the two liked each other a lot, only that they weren't cuddly cats. It was Howy who kept walking up to Flix and showing him that closeness isn't bad, that it can also be beautiful. Howy, whose happiness was contagious to all of us, cheered Flix on, showed him what joy was. I'm sure he made Flix laugh a lot!

Howy brought ease, joy, and love into Flix's life—and my life too! He was the one who, in his gentle way, changed the thoughtful, brooding, somewhat melancholy Flix. Howy never wanted to be boss, he just wanted to be part of everything, to participate. And Howy always wanted to communicate. With us and with Flix. And be heard. That was important to him. Not being the boss. With Flix it was exactly the opposite. It meant a lot to him that Howy accepted him in the role of Boss Cat, and simply accepted him for who he was with his physical limitations.

Over time, Flix realized that Howy was not a threat to him, but that he had been given a wonderful friend. He made this known early on in the animal conversations: "Howy is OK, he's just a bit exhausting sometimes." From Flix's point of view, there is no better way to sum it up.

How did Flix deal with experiencing Howy's last phase of life? Flix was tense; the situation was very stressful for him, no question about it. Howy's dying process in fact caused Flix some physical pain, in his kidneys and his stomach.

You could tell by watching Flix carry out his inspection rounds much more precisely than before. Once he got into the "flow" with his patrolling, there was no stopping him. He walked round after round, ten, twenty times in a row, without a break. The nervous twists and turns that he had experienced after the vestibular syndrome surgery increased. That too was a sign of the stress he was undergoing.

Flix couldn't even rest at night. Since Howy slept with us for the last few months, someone still had to watch over the territory. So, Flix had to make sure everything was fine downstairs at night. Howy had probably taken that on beforehand, certainly not always to Flix's complete satisfaction, but he also had a clear task there. But now he was up in bed with us.

Flix often stayed in my study at night and when he came upstairs, he just couldn't relax and crawl into his cave. No, he sat down in the doorway to the bedroom on the parquet floor so he wouldn't miss a thing.

He had to make sure that he could catch up on some sleep in the morning. Being the Boss Cat and taking care of his sick friend was exhausting. No doubt. But hey, when duty calls, you just have to answer. That was how he saw it. And anyway, if his Boss Cat duties bothered him, he didn't show it.

In mid-May Flix had a bioresonance appointment with Tom via Skype. Usually he stayed on the bed for that, sitting in front of the laptop and enjoying his appointment. Not this time. He went downstairs and started doing his rounds, one at a time. The nervous turning and twisting was apparent during nearly every round he completed.

At that appointment, Flix was given a relaxation treatment. It took almost a quarter of an hour for it to take effect. Then he finally lay down on the white carpet in my study. After a few more minutes he stretched out completely and came to rest. His breathing became calmer and deeper. Relaxation at last!

Flix was very aware of the final phase of Howy's life. I am sure that the two of them used their afternoon gatherings in the bedroom to exchange ideas and make one or two arrangements. Interestingly, when I visited both of them, Flix often came to the bed, mostly without hissing. It all felt normal. As if it had been like that forever.

On the day of Howy's death, Flix stayed up in his cave. He stopped by for a moment, but when he saw the vet, he preferred to stay safe. You never know when this could get ugly.

Only in the evening did he go to Howy, sniffed him and his bed and said goodbye in his own way. I'm sure both of them have gone through this before. In that way, Flix paid his respects, his last respects, and officially took note of Howy's departure.

From then on, Flix dealt with things himself, in his way of dealing with grief and showing us: "I have everything under control, everything is OK." He became more affectionate, spent more time with us, next to us, as long as his busy schedule permitted. He now had to take care of everything himself. He was in my study a lot, I visited him upstairs more often, and he also went into Michael's office more. Now it seemed he wanted to be picked up more often than before. Fill up on closeness, receive love and caresses. Coping with the loss of a friend. And surely he wanted to comfort us too, to help us get over Howy's death.

His need for closeness was made clear by his jumping onto the bed between five and six o'clock in the morning, and lying on top of our bellies.

Around six o'clock he left again. In the evening, he wanted to be close again, and sat with one of us on our stomachs or laps. He obviously had a lot to cope with and really missed talking to his feline partner.

Howy's death hit him too, in the truest sense of the word. In the last week of Howy's life Flix developed a so-called "kidney fur" when the fur around the kidneys looks bad. I then increased his Ren Suis[1] from once to twice a week. His next bioresonance appointment was completely dedicated to dealing with grief and the kidneys. He mourned a lot, found it difficult to let go. His bowel movements also suffered a bit and his psyche was ailing—and so were his kidneys. He was treated for all this and it was very good for him.

Flix got a new bioresonance program imprinted on globules, and I kept using his medicinal mushrooms and ampoules for his kidneys. He had been getting the Cordyceps/ABM[2] medicinal mushrooms for a long time, one capsule in the food administered throughout the day, and his Solidago. Plus one ampoule of Ren Suis once a week.

There were days when he looked content and there were days when he looked sad. His eyes always spoke volumes. On some days, it hit me right in my heart when I looked into his deep, knowing, and sad eyes. Then I just took him in my arms, which he enjoyed very much during this phase. Gradually it got better, and we comforted each other and talked about our dear Howy, whom we all missed so much. It got better, a little bit every day. For all of us.

I often had the feeling that Howy was visiting us, that he was taking care of things and looking after things. Kerstin had a conversation with Flix a few weeks after Howy's death:

———————

Dear Tamara,

I get in touch with Flix very quickly. The first thing I do is connect with his feelings. I immediately perceive the stomach very strongly. It's like the feeling when you say "That upsets my stomach."

1. Ren Suis = homeopathic remedy to strengthen kidney function
2. ABM = Agaricus Blazei Murrill is a medicinal mushroom which, among other things, stabilizes the immune system and can be used as a complementary cancer therapy.

A feeling of discomfort with pressure in the stomach area. I feel the heartbeat pulsating throughout the body.

Flix already misses Howy, but he also says that Howy isn't completely gone. He is often here and looks after everyone.

It's OK for Flix. He can manage well on his own and doesn't necessarily need a companion. But he doesn't mind if a new cat moves in, as long as they leave him alone, respect him and don't annoy him too much.

Flix says "*Howy's place is available, and I know Howy will make sure it doesn't stay unoccupied for long. I trust him, he'll make the right choice ...*"

Even if Flix and Howy were not physically close, they nonetheless have a very strong emotional connection that continues and will continue to exist now.

Each of them has always accepted the other one as he was.

Suddenly Howy is there and speaks up.

"*I know that the grief is great and takes time, but it is important not to lose sight of the future, even if it may be blurred by tears ...*"

At the same time, a colorful butterfly flutters around me briefly, turns a few laps on the terrace and then flies away ... with him Howy too ...

Once again I am sitting here with tears in my eyes because I am so touched by the conversations and the signs they send us ...

I'll come back to Flix one more time. Flix says he's fine and OK. Please don't worry. He says "*Continue your journey, one issue less to worry about. Now, you have more capacity for good thoughts and ideas that want to be implemented ...*"

Thank you Flix and Howy, you touched me deeply again.

———————

How beautiful! Typical Flix. The way that Howy cares is exactly what Max did after his death as well. How much the animals care for their humans and their friends is incredible and wonderful.

I was then very relieved to see how Flix stabilized over the next few weeks. He is an extremely great fighter. And, to be honest, as a Boss Cat you always have to set a good example.

THEY MOVED INTO OUR HEARTS

Sometimes you need a break. To be all by yourself. So did I. Just needed to be there for myself. Get a couple of issues sorted. Listen to myself. Follow my intuition. And I felt very clearly, take time for yourself. Now. Don't put it off again. Go away now. You will see why.

So, I canceled my projects for a few days and drove to the sea. To Usedom on the Baltic Sea, directly to the beach. Just for me.

Michael looked after Flix at home. So everything was fine. I had explained to Flix beforehand why I had to do this. Completely OK with him. "You're coming back," he said.

I wanted to have time for myself, to give myself space and time to grieve for Howy. I wanted to speak to him if he had time for me. And, to see where all of this would take me.

When I arrived in Usedom to stay in a small, very lovingly run hotel, I first went to the beach. It was windy and relatively cool. Exactly my weather. Take off your shoes, feel the sand and water under your feet and off you go. I enjoyed it so much, first of all just running; just letting my thoughts come and go.

The next morning, right after breakfast, I went back out to the sea, the beach, to feel the sand, feel the sea, breathe the wonderful sea air. After walking for a while, I connected with Howy's soul. I just wanted to see if he might have some time for me. And there he was. I was immediately connected to him; he was very happy and accompanied me on the beach.

How much I missed him and how happy I was to "see" him, to feel his energy! Indescribable! I could literally hear him, his distinctive Howy-meow, which always reminded you of a sheep. That's how we had fallen in love with him!

He was doing well; he was well received, spent a lot of time with Max, who showed him everything. "And yes, of course, whenever you think you can feel me, then I'll be with you and see if everything is going right. You are dealing with it perfectly, even though your grief is profound; it is with me too, you know that I had to go because my body could no longer hold on. Still, I would have loved to stay with you longer."

I was so happy, this was so fulfilling, to sense him, to feel him, to experience him, to be able to talk to him.

"You're doing it just right," he said. "By the way, what about the soul cats book? Now that I'm gone, you know what the second part of the book should be."

Yeah, yeah. After Howy came to us, the soul cats book faded into the background. I had written a lot in the months after Max's death, including about Flix's recovery. But then Howy came along. After that I barely had time. When I got back to the book every now and then, I wasn't sure how and where it should end. Should it be a Max and Flix book that ends when Howy arrived? Or should it be a Max, Flix, and Howy book?

Well, it became the latter. I finished the book in a few days in a flash. It actually wrote itself. It ends with Howy's departure. Of our three soul cats, two are now on the other side of the Rainbow Bridge. Yet they are never completely gone. Their love and joy have moved into our hearts.

Because they are connected to us far beyond death, they know exactly what is going on with us. And Howy, like Max before, will know exactly when another cat will join us again. He will know what this little soul cat should be like, so that it goes well with Flix, and signals the beginning of a new chapter for us.

We have all the confidence we need and are very excited!

But first, the story of my soul cats had to be finished and published. All three cats agreed on that.

HOWY HAS A MESSAGE

We took Howy to the same cremation service as Max. A very pleasant conversation took place this time, too. It is simply good to be able to talk about your animal, to be heard. Then there was the question of the urn. We chose a very modern urn for Max, which is very reminiscent of the silhouette of a cat. In black. When I saw the same style urn at the funeral home, the decision was made. It was going to be a gray urn for our predominantly gray tiger.

Less than a week later, Howy was back home. I put his urn next to Max's. Then I placed a tea light there with a picture imprinted on it of two cats next to each other, and lit it. Beautiful. It was perfect.

That evening, when Flix came down, he walked by as if both of them had always been there. All was good.

As you read in the previous chapter, Howy urged me to finally finish writing the soul cats book, this very book. As you can see, I finished writing *Soul Cats* in a few weeks, giving it high priority.

Howy had another message. A soul message for me and for all humans. I promised him that his message would of course be included in the book. Here it is:

Follow your soul.
Do what you are here for.
Your intuition guides you.

Let love and joy be your guiding principles.

Whatever you do, do it with love.
For all living beings.
Always.

In love and joy
Your Howy

Wow, I'm overwhelmed with love for my Howy. Thank you from the bottom of my heart, dear Howy!

I will heed your message.

Promised!

MAX ON ANIMAL SOULS
AND HUMAN SOULS

M y beloved Max commissioned this book. So, he should also have
his say about the really important things in life. On the question of
what constitutes an animal soul in comparison to a human soul. Clearly a
question for Max. For Sir Max.

I connected with him in late June 2020 and received a lesson from Max.
This is what he told me about in several conversations:

---

*Animal souls are much more similar to human souls than we would
expect. The principles are pretty much the same. Likewise, the universal
laws by which we (should) live.*

*I can give you some practical knowledge that I have learned in the
course of several incarnations as an animal.*

*We have reincarnations, as do you. I know people should actually
take their bodies with them when they die, but I've never seen it like this
before. We animals always leave our bodies behind when we die. That
may be a difference.*

*The other difference is how we are structured compared to humans.
It is often said (by humans) that we animals essentially live driven by our
first and second chakras, i.e. survival and emotions. That is not accurate.
We use our minds, but differently than you humans.*

The link for us animal souls is our instinct. We use our minds through the lens of our instinct. With human souls, everything is much more complicated, because there is what you call free will, i.e. decisions based on free will. We have that too. But both principles are implemented differently in animals than in humans.

Then of course we have a soul identity as far as I can tell. Our heart chakra is not as closed as that of humans.

If the human heart chakra were more open, we would all not have so much cruelty in the world, and not so much violence against animals and cruelty to animals.

And yes, we have a throat chakra and we have a voice. But not so many people have the ability to listen to us animals and talk to us. I assume that all people potentially have this ability, but that most of them don't use it. You always had this ability in you, but you didn't know it when we met at the shelter. I felt that in you, and that's why I immediately felt very connected to you, safe and secure. Then I did my part so that you could learn. And you did. And you've learned many other wonderful ways to help people. It's good to work on both sides.

And it will come as no surprise to anyone that we animals, especially cats, have higher senses. We perceive things differently than people, on a different frequency. This means that our perception of life is different. We perceive dangers earlier and can act accordingly. And yes, because we use our minds through the lens of our instincts.

Another big difference is that we live a lot more in the here and now. You cannot survive as an animal outside and enjoy your life if you are not in the here and now with all your senses activated. And you cannot survive if you are not at peace with yourself, if you are not in harmony with nature and everything.

When we live with people, things get more complicated. We need to learn that you make decisions differently than we do and that our lives depend on what decisions you make. It is very important to me that you humans gain a deep understanding of all of this.

Since humans tend to worry a lot, which in turn influences their emotions, we animals often have a lot of things to carry for you. We have to somehow balance it, so that at least we are in harmony with ourselves, our environment and the great entirety.

Do you understand?

Animals are usually in tune with nature, with themselves, but most humans are not. So we have to stay in our clarity while we help you so that you also reach this harmony with yourself and the environment, with nature. That is why so many animals adopt the problems, behaviors or diseases of their humans.

You learned with me what it means to live in the moment, to live in harmony. And Flix and Howy know that too. And luckily, you've learned how to resolve these issues for all of us. This is fantastic. That's why we all really became revitalized with you, even if we were all older.

When I was still with you, a lot could throw you off your balance. You were very, very vulnerable. That is now probably much better, as I can perceive. Not because you are less vulnerable, but because you are more in balance, in tune with the world. And that makes you a lot stronger. That is why I said that I would continue to accompany you, that our work was not finished when I had to leave.

That's why I used my paws just right to push you so that you adopt Howy. Howy brought with him so much joy and love and playfulness, more than I ever could have brought you. And Flix is still with you. For good reason. He is your mirror.

I guess that's all I can tell you about animal and human souls.

Please never stop helping animals and creating more understanding for animals among humans. That's why the Soul Cats Book is so important here.

I have to go now. Newcomers need me.

I can barely express what I feel.
Max's message goes very, very deep.
Tears are flowing, it's so beautiful.
I thank you from the bottom of my heart, dear Max, you wonderful soul! I love you more than anything, across space and time.

Of course I promise you that, dear Max, and all animals!
I will never stop helping animals and bringing humans closer to animals, in their complexity, in their wisdom, in their uniqueness, in their wholeness as wonderful living beings on an equal footing.

This is how Max, Flix, and Howy taught me to navigate with the heart.

AFTERWORD—JULY 2021

I hope you enjoyed our story so far, and I also hope that we inspired and entertained you in one way or another. I know we covered quite a lot, and some chapters were emotional, heavy, and more challenging to digest than others.

Now, I am sure that you are probably wondering whether Flix got a new cat friend or not, and how he is doing. Reading an Afterword at a point where just one of my beautiful soul cats remained might make you feel a bit sad before even reading this last part of our story.

I'd love to encourage you to hold love in your heart, trust the process, and don't be sad. Rather, be pleased at how deeply connected Flix and I were, how our relationship became even more intense, and how he mastered the rest of his life. And, of course, be impressed with what assignments I received from him! Be assured he thought everything through to the smallest detail.

Ready to continue? Beautiful!

After publishing my book in Germany in September 2020, Flix and I were running straight into the next kidney crisis. Kidney crisis, Take 3, so to say. It was in October, exactly one year after the second kidney crisis you just read about in the book. Flix had a kidney and blood pressure check-up appointment in the clinic with our usual vet. Unfortunately, his kidney results were not good, to say the least. Instead, they were rather alarming.

The alternatives were to keep him in the clinic for a few days or administer subcutaneous fluids at home.

As you read about the tremendous stress he experienced being in the clinic with kidney crisis Take 2, you can imagine that the clinic wasn't even an option for me. No, now was the time to learn how to administer subcutaneous fluids at home. My vet took the time to explain everything in great detail, all the utensils I'd need, and how to best administer the fluids. She demonstrated it to me on Flix, and then it was my turn to practice. And yes, Flix cooperated nicely and I managed it. What a relief!

From that moment on until one month before his transition, I administered daily fluids this way. Flix wasn't particularly pleased with the process, but he accepted it and sensed that it was helpful for him. We started with only 50 ml per day as Flix was a small cat. Soon after we started this process, he became fitter, ate a bit better, and felt better.

At the same time, I felt guided to think about adding another senior cat to our family. We checked out the cats at the animal shelter in Hanau, where Howy came from. I felt connected immediately to a black and white female cat, a few years younger than Flix. However, when I wanted to make an appointment, she had already found a new home. And the same happened with two other cats I felt connected to. I sensed it was not the right time for us to add another cat to the family. I spoke to Flix about it, and he clearly stated that he would now prefer to stay the only cat with us for the rest of his life. We would need the time together, he said. Right on.

Between Christmas and January 6, I attended an online workshop for humans and their animals that guided us through the Twelfthtide. If you've never heard about it, let me share more about this European tradition. Twelfthtide includes the twelve nights between December 25 and January 6. It's said that during these nights you can have a special connection to the spirits. That was a fascinating process, especially the work with the animals. Cat conversations happened every night regarding different topics. When we had to talk about the year 2021 with our cats, Flix was very clear that he would be transitioning in 2021. He wasn't afraid of anything; he was relatively clear and calm about the process, the coming end of his incarnation, and the time we would have together until then. It wasn't easy to process for me, although I was, of course, aware that he would turn 21 years old and was really a super senior boy with a severe CKD and a silent vestibular syndrome. We would make the best out of it!

However, accompanying an old animal during the last phase of his life is never a comfort zone. But it's absolutely worth it, as it is a growth zone.

The last six months of our time together can be summarized with: "Surrender, trust, love, acceptance" and "Less is more." And all this required both of us to let go of old structures, concepts, and ideas on how things should be. Also a complete letting go of what was "right" or "wrong." Transitioning is a very individual process and different for every living being. Surrender and trusting the process were at the top of the list.

Early in 2021, Flix started to refuse his blood pressure pills. First, he only took it every other day, and then he stopped taking the pills altogether. At the same time, he made clear that the higher amount of daily fluids didn't help him either. So, we reduced the fluids back to 50 ml per day. Of course, I investigated that and talked to him. Here is an excerpt from my animal communication from late March 2021 with Flix (you can read the full article on my blog …):

———————

Do you have some time for me, dear Flix?

"Sure. Always."

How are you doing, dear Flix?

"Well, as good as it can be at this stage of my life. You know everything, my damaged kidneys, my back, my teeth … it is what it is. It's a part of my journey."

Yes, I feel it, with a heavy heart. My heart feels like a big, heavy rock. It's Flix' heart that I feel. We feel the same way.

This last phase of his life is very intense. Beautifully intense. Also very touching, because everything comes now to the surface. It's not a comfort zone, but a learning and growth zone. For both of us.

If you love your animal friend so much you avoid thinking about the time when his soul will have left his body. However, you should walk this journey together as consciously as you possibly can. In love. In trust. With lots of time together.

You know that I want to keep you pain-free, as best as I can.

"Yes, I know, and that's lovely. But I don't need anything else anymore. It wouldn't change anything, and I cannot process more of anything. You see?"

Yes, I understand, dear Flix. And I will support you as you want to be supported. However, please let me know if you need anything else, whatever it is. Just let me know.

"Sure, will do! If I cannot stand it anymore, you will feel it."

Sure, I will. My dear boy, I love you so much.

"Yes, I love you, too. Without you, I wouldn't even be here right now. I am very grateful that you always believed in me. If not, I wouldn't have recovered from surgery years ago. I wouldn't be the cat I became this way. I will never forget this."

I feel tears on my cheeks … simply because my heart has so much more to say. And also, because most things between us are said and done.

I also became another person due to you being you, dear Flix. You always believed in me, such as now, where so many things are changing in my life. I always feel you saying, *"Walk your path regardless of how many iterations it will have. It's your journey, your mission. If you can help humans to open their hearts, you also help us animals, and you help us animals anyway. Your work is essential. Just do it."*

Promised, I will launch my new program, "Empower Your True Potential" in May.

"That's amazing! Do it, whether or not I am physically here. I will always be with you."

Thanks so much, dear Flix! We are so deeply connected.

"Yes, and that will always be the case, across space and time."

Thanks for your wisdom, dear Flix.

We cuddled a bit, and then I went back to my desk, deeply touched and moved, full of love for my dear Flix. Onwards and upwards with my soul's mission to help people clear blockages, discover their soul potential and finally live it.

My heavy heart was gone …

A few weeks later, Flix had decided to not take any medication at all any longer. We only continued the daily fluids. He stayed now in the bedroom most of the time. Walking on the stairs only happened very rarely; he stopped it the end of May completely. He lost weight, not because he was a bad eater but because his body couldn't make good use of the food anymore.

In the last week of May, he stopped the fluids and we had quite an incident on our journey together. It all came at once, so let's discuss one after the other.

Flix was in the process of deciding whether he wanted to continue the fluids or not. I was a bit nervous; he said he wasn't sure and wanted us to offer it a few more times. Each time, it was a no. OK, we are done with the fluids. And now, what?

I assumed that without the fluids, his life would end within a few days. However, that was not the case. Interestingly, he managed it pretty well, as he finally stopped eating the small amounts of dry food he received as treats (you remember he came as a dry food junkie). As soon as the fluids ended, he stopped eating these. Amazing. He managed well and found a new balance, now with only wet food and fresh water. And he did relatively well, given his overall condition as a 21-year-old cat in the last stage of his life.

The incident I mentioned happened at the same time, one of the last attempts to offer fluids. He walked away and wobbled around. He could barely walk and had a severe issue with his sense of balance. Another acute vestibular syndrome? And he had a hard time orienting himself. Did he go blind in that very moment? Severe movement disorders and strange looking eyes. It was a Friday evening, and luckily Tom could help us the next day.

His eyes were clear the following day. Luckily! We learned that his movement disorders came from the degeneration of a part of his brain that controlled his movements. We rearranged things for him, put a second litter box in front of the bedroom, and kept the other one in the bathroom. We also secured the stairs to prevent him from falling down.

We were definitely living through his last days. At this point, I was very grateful to have Martina with me, supporting me with excellent animal communications with Flix, as I was much too involved emotionally.

These conversations with another, more neutral person for him, were also crucial for Flix, as he could share his perspectives and communicate his assignment for me: writing another book, the book about Flix and my journey of finding our soul missions and supporting each other, while working on our shared trauma, fears, and worries.

He reflected on his life, connected the dots to other incarnations, and was happy with his accomplishments and having met his big human love, me. He said that he had taken things for me into his paws for the last six-and-a-half years, and that I could now continue my journey on my own.

Could you ever ask for more?

He accepted a pain killer for the last few weeks of his life. He was pleased about it at this point. However, the day came when he became weaker and weaker, and said that everything was completed and that he wanted to cross over in the coming night.

Also, the fact that his body increasingly refused to follow his commands was very disturbing for Flix. No, he had planned differently. His level of surrender was challenged and we were both asked to let go again of old structures and concepts about how things should be.

If he couldn't transition tonight, he said, he would appreciate help on the next day. As everything was completed between us, there was no reason for staying in this body that didn't follow his commands any longer, he stated.

"Any last wishes, dear Flix?"

"Yes, an auric clearing with Tamara," he said to Martina, and sitting one last time on the balcony with me in the evening. We started doing this after the crisis in May every evening, when we sought some fresh air outside, Flix in my arms, enjoying the fresh air.

It was Monday, June 21. I processed his last auric clearing for him, with tears in my eyes. He enjoyed it a lot and relaxed in his cat bed.

The following day, Martina asked him again if his wish was still the same. *"Sure, I said so."*

I called the mobile vet, whom I had informed a few days ago that we might soon require their help. She was supposed to come around 11 am. Due to an emergency, she came shortly after 1 pm.

Which was a gift. We had the entire morning together, listening to the Om Mane Padme Hum meditation, talking and cuddling, with Martina on the telepathic line with us. Absolutely beautiful. When the vet arrived, he was already on his way; he only needed the anesthesia then he was gone. It was June 22, 2021.

Thank you so much, dear Flix, for our precious time together, and especially for the last year. I don't want to miss a single moment of our given time. You taught me so much; especially navigating with the heart, you could find your way and you made sure that I follow my mission.

Our love is a timeless bond at the soul level.

PS: A few weeks after he transitioned, Michael and I were at the Baltic Sea for vacation. One day, on the beach, I connected with Flix and we had a lovely chat. I was so happy to feel him and talk to him and hear that he was happy. He had found his previous human who passed away before we met him at the shelter, and of course, Max and Howy and his broader soul family.

I also asked him if he would send us feline souls again, in divine right timing. He said *"They are already there."*

I only understood a few weeks later what he meant. I found myself offering a home for cats in need after so many lost their homes during the floods in Germany in July 2021.

At the end of July, Hubertus and Joey, 16 and 11 years old, moved in with us. They lost their human and were already alone for about five weeks, cared for on an emergency basis. Another of Flix' assignments.

Both are beautiful souls, and Flix also assigned a specific challenge to me: healing trauma for humans and animals. It should become a core aspect of my work.

Find more here:

https://energyfieldmastery.com/

https://soul-cats.com

ABOUT THE AUTHOR

Author, Mentor, Energetic
Healer and Connector,
Entrepreneur

Author Tamara Schenk owes her passion
for writing to her soul cat Max. Max, in his
divine feline wisdom, knew that his human
guardian loved to write. That intuition is
what helped to influence Tamara to write
Soul Cats with the right divine timing.

Tamara Schenk is the founder of Energy Field Mastery, where she works
together with humans (as well as their animals) to deeply cleanse and purify
auric, karmic, and soul level blockages. As these blockages are often the
root of so many challenges, Tamara's process is cultivated from the ground
up to reconnect humans with their soul insights and purpose and reignite
their true potential.

She is a highly recognized thought leader and speaker in the field of
sales enablement, as a director at Bartlett Schenk & Company. Tamara has
repeatedly demonstrated a deep mastery of re-energizing people and setting
a fire within their hearts.

In *Soul Cats*, Tamara speaks through the experiences of Max, Flix, and
Howy and how they all helped Tamara to find her mission—to empower
humans to live out their soul's potential and heal the human-animal relationship on the planet.

RESOURCES

After you've read the story of Max, Flix, and Howy, you might want to find out more, because one of your cats may also need appropriate treatment.

Here you will find some useful information and further links. This information does not claim to be complete. They are sources that have helped me a lot.

Chronical Kidney Disease (CKD):

- Tanya's Comprehensive Guide to Feline Chronic Kidney Disease: (in my opinion the most comprehensive guide out there) https://www .felinecrf.org/
- The Ins and Outs of Managing Feline Chronic Kidney Disease: https://todaysveterinarynurse.com/articles/managing-feline-chronic -kidney-disease/
- Feline Chronic Kidney Disease: https://todaysveterinarypractice.com /feline-chronic-kidney-disease/
- Traditional Chinese Veterinary Medicine for Renal Failure: https://www .vin.com/apputil/content/defaultadv1.aspx?id=7259169&pid=14365
- Medicinal Mushrooms for Animals: https://mykotroph.de/en /animals-medicinal-mushrooms/

- Facebook "Cats with Chronic Renal Failure Support Group": https://www.facebook.com/groups/190072827795180

FORL:

- Feline odontoclastic resorptive lesion: https://en.wikipedia.org/wiki/Feline_odontoclastic_resorptive_lesion
- Feline Tooth Resorption: https://todaysveterinarypractice.com/practical-dentistry-feline-tooth-resorption/

Vestibular syndrome:

- Vestibular Disease in Cats: https://www.thesprucepets.com/treating-vestibular-disease-in-cats-5082137
- Vestibular Syndrome in Dogs and Cats Fact Sheet: https://vetspecialists.co.uk/fact-sheets-post/vestibular-syndrome-in-dogs-and-cats-fact-sheet/
- Vestibular Disease in Cats: https://vcahospitals.com/know-your-pet/feline-vestibular-disease

Soul Cats Online:

- Internet: https://soul-cats.com/
- Facebook: https://www.facebook.com/MySoulCats/